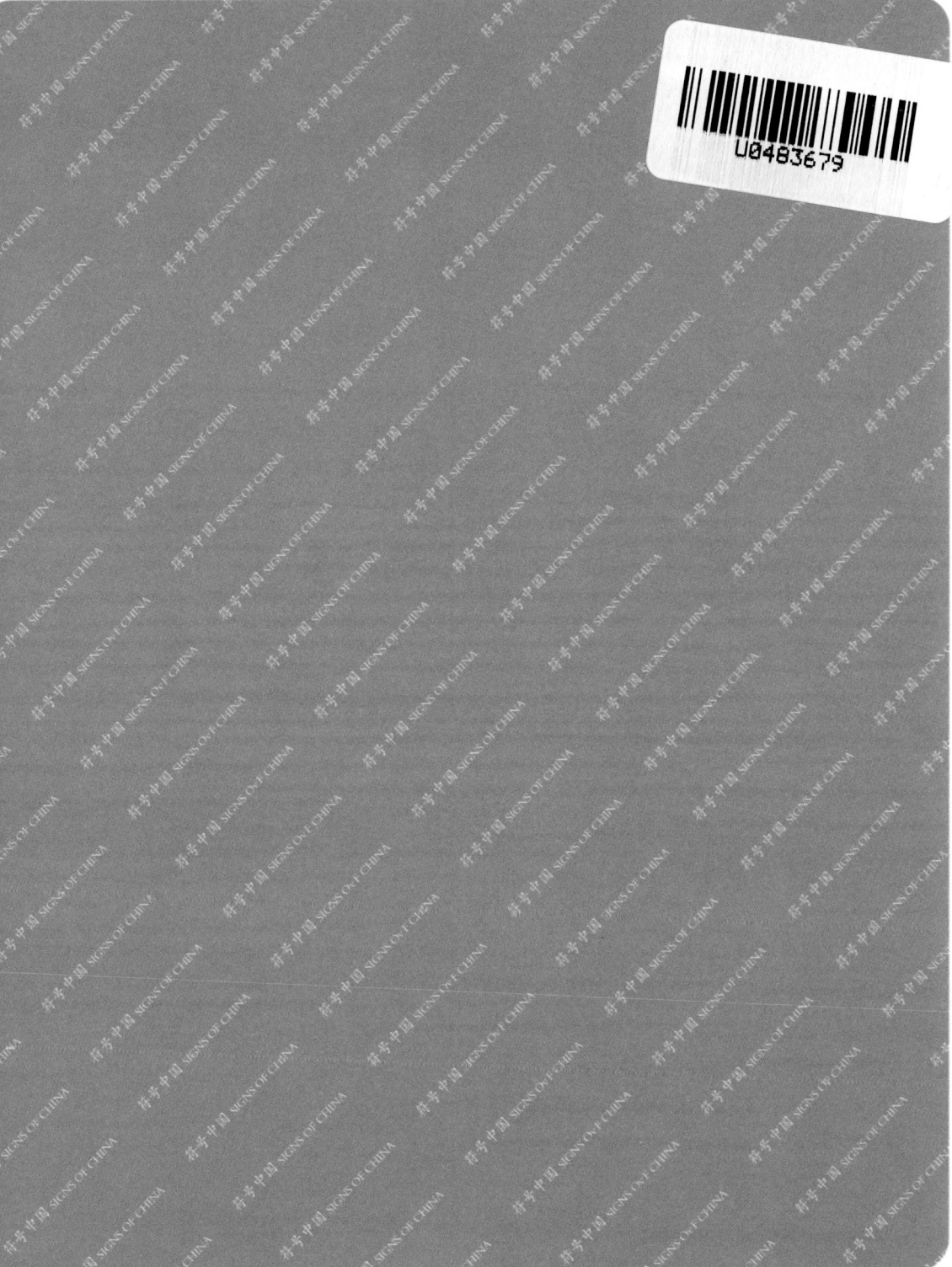

符号中国 SIGNS OF CHINA

汉 字
CHINESE CHARACTERS

"符号中国"编写组 ◎ 编著

中央民族大学出版社
China Minzu University Press

图书在版编目(CIP)数据

汉字：汉文、英文 /"符号中国"编写组编著. —北京：中央民族大学出版社，2024.8
（符号中国）
ISBN 978-7-5660-2352-0

Ⅰ.①汉… Ⅱ.①符… Ⅲ.①汉字—介绍—汉、英 Ⅳ.①H12

中国国家版本馆CIP数据核字（2024）第017447号

符号中国：汉字　CHINESE CHARACTERS

编　　著	"符号中国"编写组
策划编辑	沙　平
责任编辑	杨爱新
英文指导	李瑞清
英文编辑	邱　械
美术编辑	曹　娜　郑亚超　洪　涛
出版发行	中央民族大学出版社
	北京市海淀区中关村南大街27号　　邮编：100081
	电话：（010）68472815（发行部）　传真：（010）68933757（发行部）
	（010）68932218（总编室）　　　　（010）68932447（办公室）
经 销 者	全国各地新华书店
印 刷 厂	北京兴星伟业印刷有限公司
开　　本	787 mm×1092 mm　1/16　印张：9.5
字　　数	136千字
版　　次	2024年8月第1版　2024年8月第1次印刷
书　　号	ISBN 978-7-5660-2352-0
定　　价	58.00元

版权所有　侵权必究

"符号中国"丛书编委会

唐兰东　巴哈提　杨国华　孟靖朝　赵秀琴

本册编写者

师　妓

前言 Preface

在2008年北京奥运会开幕式上，中国向世界展示了历史悠久、博大精深、丰富多彩的中华文明。897位开幕式表演者操作着897块活字印刷字块变换出不同字体的"和"字，向世界传达了中国"和为贵"的传统思想，同时形象地展现了中国汉字的历史发展进程。

中国的汉字与苏美尔人的楔形文字、埃及的象形文字同为世界上最为

At the opening ceremony of the 2008 Beijing Olympic Games, China presented to the world a palace of civilization, long-standing, profound and colorful. There, 897 moveable-type blocks powered by 897 performers bounced up and down, spelling out the character "和" (harmony) in different fonts, which conveyed the Chinese traditional value of "peace is most preaous" to the whole world, and meanwhile vividly demonstrated the historical evolution of Chinese characters.

　　The Chinese character, Sumerian cuneiform and Egyptian hieroglyphics are the world's most ancient writing systems. But among all the three, only Chinese characters are still in use, carrying on the Chinese civilization of five thousand years' history. Different from any other writings in the world, Chinese character as a mature pictogram system has its own features. First, it is squarely shaped and hence also known as "square-block character". Second,

1

古老的文字。而汉字是其中唯一至今仍在使用的文字，承载着中华文明五千年的悠久历史。作为一套具有成熟体系的表意文字系统，汉字不同于世界上任何一种文字，具有独特的性质：拥有方方正正的方块式结构，因此又被称为"方块字"；使用汉语拼音的方式注音；书写时讲究笔画顺序，遵循一定的规则；有六种造字原理，即象形、指事、会意、形声、转注、假借；在漫长的历史发展中，演变出多种字体，包括小篆、隶书、草书、楷书、行书等。中国书法、篆刻、诗歌、对联等传统艺术形式则展现了汉字富于变化的形体和极富韵律的节奏。在世界文明中，汉字散发着独一无二的璀璨光芒。

本书通过对汉字的历史、汉字的特点以及书法、篆刻、诗歌、对联等中国传统文化的介绍，向读者展现中国文字的精髓。

phonetic notation takes the form of *Pinyin* (Chinese Romanization). Third, there are rules for stroke order in writing. Fourth, the formation of Chinese character can be varied from pictographic character (*Xiangxing*), self-explanatory character (*Zhishi*), associative compound character (*Huiyi*), pictophonetic character (*Xingsheng*), mutually explanatory character (*Zhuanzhu*) and phonetic loan character (*Jiajie*). Fifth, in the long history of evolution, a variety of styles have come into being, such as small seal script, clerical script, cursive script, regular script, running script, etc. Besides, Chinese calligraphy, seal carving, poetry, couplet and other traditional art forms all manifest the varied structure of Chinese characters and its beauty in rhythm. Even in the world civilization, the Chinese character emits unique brilliance.

This book mainly introduces the history and features of Chinese characters. It also refers to calligraphy, seal carving, poetry, couplets and other related traditional Chinese culture to reveal the essence of Chinese characters.

目 录 | Contents

悠久的汉字
The Long History of Chinese Characters 001

汉字的起源
The Origin of Chinese Characters 002

汉字的发展
The Evolution of Chinese Characters 007

神奇的汉字
The Magical Chinese Characters 021

汉字的注音
The Phonetic System of Chinese Characters .. 022

汉字的构形
The Structure of Chinese Characters 027

汉字的字义
The Semantic Meaning of
Chinese Characters 035

汉字造字法
The Formation of Chinese Characters 042

优美的汉字
The Graceful Chinese Characters 053

汉字与书法
Chinese Characters and Calligraphy 054

汉字与篆刻
Chinese Characters and Seal Carving 085

汉字与诗歌
Chinese Characters and Poetry 107

汉字与对联
Chinese Characters and Chinese Couplets 117

附录
Appendix 125

汉字书写工具
Writing Tools of Chinese Characters 126

如何写汉字
How to Write Chinese Characters 135

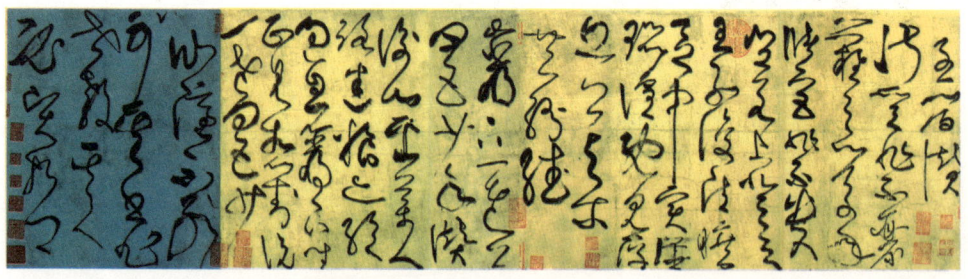

悠久的汉字
The Long History of Chinese Characters

　　汉字，亦称"中国字""中文字""方块字"，是记录中国语言的一种文字，属于表意文字的词素音节文字，是中华文明的重要标志之一。汉字是世界上使用人口最多、使用范围最广、使用时间最长的文字，其与古埃及象形文字圣书字、两河流域苏美尔人的楔形文字一样属于世界上最古老的文字，也是唯一迄今仍被使用的文字体系。

The Chinese character (*Hanzi*), also known as the Chinese word, the Chinese script or the square-block character, is a writing system of the Chinese people. It is ideographic and morpheme-syllabic, serving as one of the important symbols of Chinese civilization. Moreover, the Chinese character is the most populous, most widely and longest used writing system in the world. Besides, unlike the ancient Egyptian hieroglyphics written on the holy books, and the Sumerian cuneiform born at Mesopotamia, the Chinese character is not only most ancient, but still in current use.

> 汉字的起源

考古学家在新石器时代后期的山东大汶口文化遗址（约前4500—前2500）发现了刻有符号的陶尊和残器片，这些符号被专家们普遍认为具备简单文字的特征，是中国的原始文字。在仰韶文化（约前5000—前3000）早期的陕西半坡遗址中，出土了大量彩陶，上面绘有人面、鱼、鹿、植物枝叶及几何形等纹样，其中鱼形纹被认为与早期象形字有很大关系。

> The Origin of Chinese Characters

At Dawenkou Cultural sites of the late Neolithic Age (ca.4500 B.C.-2500 B.C.) archaeologists have found fragments of pottery vessels engraved with symbols. As the symbols reveal features of simple script, experts generally regarded them as ancient Chinese characters. Later at the Banpo Sites of Shaanxi Province were unearthed many painted potteries made in the early period of Yangshao Culture (ca.5000 B.C.-3000 B.C.). There we can see decorated patterns of human face, fish, deer, branch and leaf of plant, and geometric forms, among which the

• 人面鱼纹盆（仰韶文化）
Basin with Human Face and Fish Design
(Yangshao Culture, ca.5000 B.C.-3000 B.C.)

新石器时代

　　新石器时代是考古学上石器时代的最后一个阶段，与旧石器时代相对应。这一时期，人类开始使用磨制石器，并创造了彩陶，是人类社会物质文明发展的一个重要阶段。中国的新石器时代距今约1万年，最早出现在黄河流域和长江流域。仰韶文化、龙山文化是新石器时代的历史代表。

Neolithic Age

In archeological chronology, the Neolithic Age (ca.10,000-4000 years ago), corresponding to the Paleolithic Period (ca.1,700,000-10,000 years ago), is the last phase of the Stone Age. During this period, human beings began to use polished stone implement and also created painted pottery. It is an important stage in the development of material civilization. The Chinese Neolithic Age appeared circa 10,000 years ago at the Yellow and Yantze rivers. Yangshao Culture and Longshan Culture are representative of this historical period.

- 龙山文化黑陶高柄杯
  Black Pottery Cup with High Stem in Longshan Culture (ca.2800 B.C.-2300 B.C.)

- 仰韶文化船形网纹彩陶壶
  Boat-shaped Painted Pot with Net Pattern in Yangshao Culture (ca.5000 B.C.-3000 B.C.)

汉字产生之前，古人用结绳记事的方式来记录日常生活，结绳即将绳子打结，通过绳结的大小、数量来记录所发生的事情。刻木记事，也是原始记事方法之一。古人在竹子、木头上刻上不同大小、不同样式的符号来记录日常生活。但是，这种原始的记事方法，只能满足人们记录简单事件的要求，不能

fish pattern is considered to be strongly related with the early pictographs.

Before the generation of Chinese characters, the ancients would tie knots into different sizes and numbers to keep daily records, or by wood notching which is another way to set down everyday life. Usually they would notch symbols of different sizes and styles on bamboos or woods, but for all practical purposes, such ancient methods can only help to record simple events. As the need arose for more communication, ancient people

- **结绳记事**

  这是原始先民以绳结形式反映客观经济活动及其数量关系的记录方式，是在文字产生之前古人广泛使用的记录方式之一。

  Keep Records by Tying Knots

  In ancient China, people usually tied knots to record economic activities and denote quantitative relations. This method is widely used before the generation of characters.

满足人们沟通、交流更多信息的需要，于是先民们开始探索另外一种交流信息的工具。随着人类社会的发展，结绳、刻木因为不能适应范围大、数量多的记事要求而遭到淘汰，渐渐地产生了图画文字、符号文字等原始汉字的雏形。图画文字由直观、形象、写实的图画演化而来，通过多次使用产生相应的联系，具有某种约定性，从而在使用过程中达到消息互通的效果。由图画文字发展变化来的符号文字产生于公元前1万年左右，可以说是中国远古时代最初的文字。

began to explore a better channel to exchange information. Thus since the demand of social development went beyond the range of knot-tying and wood-notching, some pictographs and symbols gradually emerged to meet the needs; they are the early forms of Chinese characters. Pictographs are evolved from visual and realistic images. Their inter-connection is established through repeated use which in turn helps to facilitate communication in practice. The symbols, born around 10,000 B.C., are developed from pictographic writings. They are the prototype of Chinese characters in ancient times.

仓颉造字

关于汉字的产生，不得不提到"仓颉造字"的传说，这一传说最早出现在战国时期的文献《吕氏春秋》中。传说仓颉是约公元前2500年轩辕黄帝时期的史官。他从辨析鸟兽足迹中得到启发，用图画法创立了文字，又因为其从事史官的工作，需要集中使用文字对历史进行记录，因此对流传于先民中的字符加以搜集、整理和使用。所谓"仓颉造字"的历史传说曲折地反映出先民造字的历史过程。仓颉被中国人尊奉为"造字圣人"。

Cangjie, the Inventor of Chinese Characters

Based on the legend, Cangjie played a crucial role in the generation of Chinese characters. This legend first appeared in *Mister Lv's Spring and Autumn Annals* (*Lvshi Chunqiu*), a literary document of the Warring States Period (475 B.C.-221 B.C.). There Cangjie was claimed to be an official historian of the Emperor Huang about 2500 B.C. and later revered as the Great Inventor of Chinese Characters. From the footprint of birds and animals, he found inspiration for pictographs and hieroglyphics. Moreover, as his work needed words to record history, Cangjie began to collect and collate characters spread among the ancients and put them into use, just as the legend goes. In brief, Cangjie has made a significant contribution to the development of Chinese characters.

- 仓颉造字
  Cangjie, the Inventor of Chinese Characters

> 汉字的发展

从公元前2000年开始，汉字开始进入字符积累阶段。汉字的发展演变过程大致可分为甲骨文、金文、篆书、隶书、楷书等五个阶段。

现存最早的汉字是殷商时期（前1600—前1046）的甲骨文，它是一套具有比较严密的系统性的

- 刻有甲骨文的龟背
  Oracle-bone Inscriptions Incised on Turtle Shell

> The Evolution of Chinese Characters

In around 2000 B.C., Chinese characters began to enter the stage of accumulation. Its evolution can be broadly divided into five stages, oracle-bone inscriptions, bronze inscription, seal script, clerical script and regular script.

The oracle-bone inscriptions of the Shang Dynasty (1600 B.C.-1046 B.C.) are the earliest Chinese characters existent. The rigorous writing system, dating back over 3000 years, is developed from the early ideographic symbols. "Oracle-bone inscriptions", as the name suggests, are characters incised on animal bones or turtle shells, used in the palace of the late Shang Dynasty for divination or recording. It was only discovered by the end of the 19th century. Since oracle-bone inscriptions are hieroglyphics evolved from pictographic writing, in the early Shang Dynasty it more resembles

文字体系，距今约有3000多年的历史，是由早期的表意符号发展演变而来的。"甲骨文"的名称来源于商朝后期宫廷内进行占卜记事的龟甲、兽骨上的记文。在19世纪末，这些刻在龟甲、兽骨上的文字才被人们发现。由于甲骨文是从图画文字演变而成的象形文字，商代早期的甲骨文象形成分较多，直到商代晚期形声字的比例才逐渐增加。现在，发现的甲骨文有5000多字，其中1000多字已经能够被确切地辨认。甲骨文的发现对于研究汉字的产生有重要意义。

在甲骨文之后，金文逐渐产

pictographs. Only towards the late Shang Dynasty, does the proportion of phono-semantic compounds gradually increase. Now, more than 5000 oracle-bone inscriptions have been unearthed, among which 1000 characters can be clearly identified. In all, the discovery of oracle-bone inscriptions has great significance for our study of the generation of Chinese characters.

Following the steps of oracle-bone inscriptions, the bronze inscription gradually emerged. During the Shang and Zhou dynasties (1600 B.C.-256 B.C.), bronze wares came into fashion. Instruments like bell and ritual articles like *Ding* (Cauldron) were often inscribed

• 殷商时期的甲骨文
Oracle-bone Inscriptions of the Shang Dynasty (1600 B.C.-1046 B.C.)

• 毛公鼎（西周）
Bronze *Ding* of Duke Mao (Western Zhou Dynasty, 1046 B.C.-771 B.C.)

生。"金文"得名于后人是从青铜器上发现这一类型的文字的。商周时期盛行青铜器，以钟为代表的乐器和以鼎为代表的礼器类青铜器上常刻铸有文字，因此金文亦称"钟鼎文"。按照时间顺序，金文分为殷商金文、西周（前1046—前771）金文、东周（前770—前256）金文和秦汉金文。最有代表性的是西周时期的青铜器铭文，载字499个的毛公鼎是其中最为典型的代表。毛公鼎上的金文风格奇逸，结体方长，

with characters; hence bronze inscription is also known as "Script on Bell and Ding". Chronologically, the development of bronze inscription can be divided into four periods, bronze inscription of the Shang Dynasty (1600 B.C.-1046 B.C.), Western Zhou Dynasty (1046 B.C.-771 B.C.), Eastern Zhou Dynasty (770 B.C.-256 B.C.), Qin and Han dynasties (221 B.C.-220 A.D.). Among others, bronze inscription of the Western Zhou Dynasty is the most representative. One masterpiece is the *Maogong Ding*

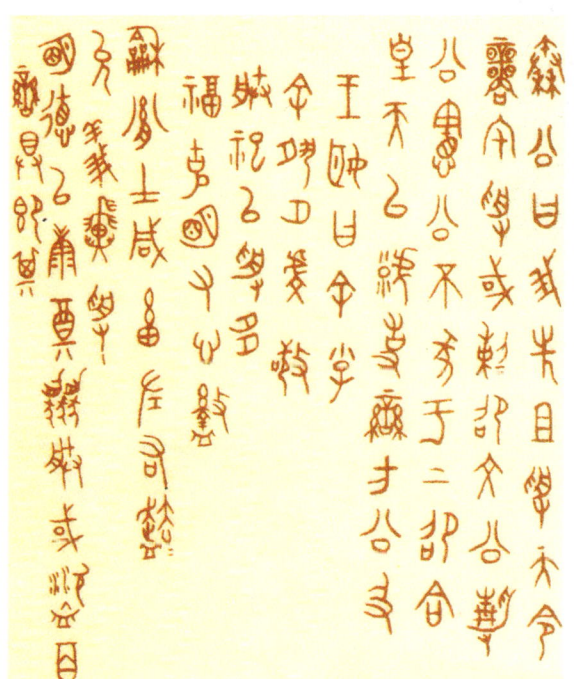

• 秦公钟金文（春秋 秦）

（图片提供：FOTOE）

Bronze Inscription on the Bell Made for Duke Qin (State of Qin in Spring and Autumn Period,770 B.C-476 B.C)

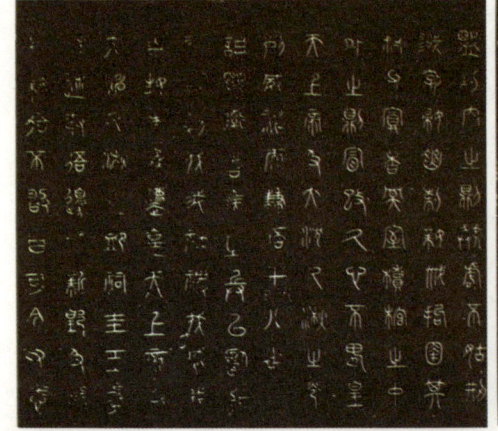
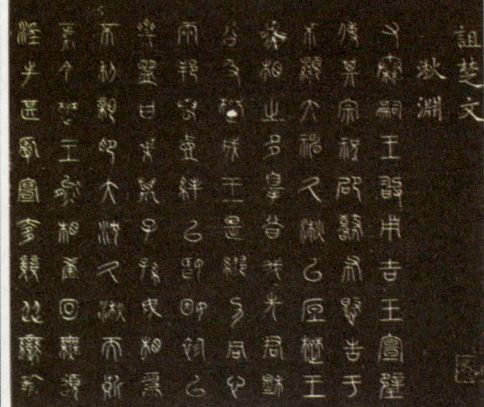
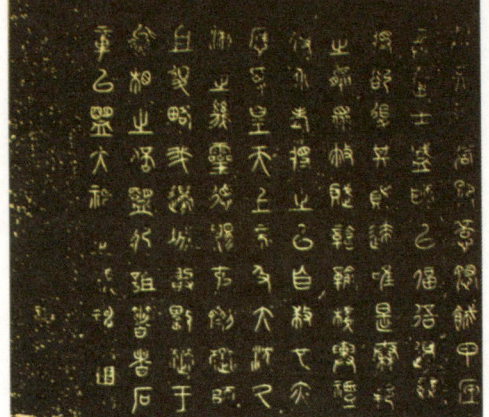

- 石刻文字"诅楚文"（战国 秦）

  秦楚两国在战国后期争夺霸权，这篇文章的内容是秦王祈求上天保佑秦国获胜，诅咒楚国败亡。石鼓文比金文规范、严正，但仍在一定程度上保留了金文的特征。

  Stone Inscription "Curse on the State of Chu" (State of Qin in Warring States Period, 475 B.C.-221 B.C.)

  In the late Warring States Period, the State of Qin and State of Chu battled for hegemony. This article is written to pray for the triumph of Qin and defeat of Chu. Stone drum script retains certain feature of the bronze inscription, but appears more standard and principled in form.

engraved with 499 characters. Oblong in structure, the bronze inscriptions outshine in style, pouring forth unaffected vigor and integrity. Hence seal script of the Zhou Dynasty (1046 B.C.-256 B.C.) has always been regarded as lineal descent of it.

The large seal script is a transitional writing form that goes between the bronze inscription and the small seal script. In the Warring States Period (475 B.C.-221 B.C.) people in the State of Qin adopted *Zhouwen* as their characters. Originated in the late Western Zhou Dynasty, this kind of script resembles small seal script in style, but has overlapping structures. Meanwhile, the other six states Qi, Chu, Yan, Han,

• 石鼓文 弘一法师（近代）

石鼓文为大篆向小篆过渡的文字，被后世学篆书的写作者奉为正宗，此帖为弘一法师临习的作品。

Stone Drum Script, by Master Hongyi (Modern Times)

Stone drum script is a transitional writing form between the large seal script and small seal script. Later calligraphers of seal script all regard it as orthodox school. This copybook is a work by Master Hongyi.

气象浑穆，笔意圆劲茂隽，历来被视为周代（前1046—前256）篆文的正宗。

大篆是上承金文、下启小篆的过渡文字。战国时期（前475—前221）的秦国，通行起源于西周晚期的籀文，其字体与小篆相近，但字形的构形多重叠。除秦国之外的六国，即齐国、楚国、燕国、韩国、赵国和魏国，则使用六国文字，又称"六国古文"。这一时期的石鼓文是大篆留传后世、保存比较完整且字数较多的书迹之一。石鼓文是刻于岩石上的石刻文字，因岩石形似鼓，故称"石鼓文"。石鼓文有中国"石刻之祖"的美誉，被奉为

Zhao and Wei persisted with their own language, known as "Ancient Script of the Six States". To have a glimpse of the large seal script, we may turn to the stone drum script of this period, well-preserved with many characters. Stone drum script is carved on drum-shaped rocks and thus gets its name. It is "the oldest known stone inscription" in China, also revered as the first rule for calligraphers. Given its high historical and artistic value, stone drum script is really worth collecting.

After Qin Shihuang (literally the First Emperor of Qin) unified China and founded the Qin Dynasty (221 B.C.-206 B.C.), one of his great policies is "to standardize Chinese scripts". He further simplified and collated the large seal

书家第一法则，具有很高的文史价值和艺术收藏价值。

秦始皇统一中国，创立了秦朝（前221—前206）。他推行的"书同文"政策，使得文字在大篆的基础上进一步简化、整理，创造了小篆这一统一的汉字书写字体。小篆也称"秦篆"，成为秦代官方的通用文字。从大篆到小篆的文字变革在中国文字史上具有重大的意义，标志着汉字向简明化、规范化的方向发展。

另外，秦代已产生了非官方的书写字体隶书。西汉（前206—公元25）末年，隶书逐渐取代了书写复杂的小篆，在全国通用。隶书比小

script, created the small seal script (also known as "Qin seal script") and made it official throughout all the conquered regions, forming one communication system over China. The transformation from large seal script to small seal script is of great importance to the development of Chinese characters, marking that Chinese writing system is moving towards the direction of simplicity and regularity.

Besides, the clerical script emerged as an unofficial style in the Qin Dynasty. By the end of the Western Han Dynasty, due to its regular and simple written style, clerical script gradually replaced the complicated small seal script and came to common use. Generally, the clerical script undergoes two periods of development. Proto-clerical script was originated in the Warring States Period (475 B.C.-221 B.C.) and further refined in the Qin Dynasty, marking an important

- 十二字砖（秦）

秦代字砖是秦代都城宫殿所用，正面为刻铸的十二个小篆文字。

Brick Incised with Twelve Characters (Qin Dynasty, 221 B.C.-206 B.C.)

The inscribed brick is used to decorate the palace in the capital city of the State of Qin. It has twelve small seal characters carved in the front side.

书同文

公元前221年之前，处于春秋战国时期的列国文字并不一致，同一种文字也有不同的写法，各诸侯国之间的交流存在一定的障碍。公元前221年，秦始皇平定中原、统一六国之后，采取了一系列治国措施，其中就包括统一文字的"书同文"政策。

秦始皇命令丞相李斯（约前284—前208，秦代著名的政治家、文学家、书法家）等人对文字进行统一整理。李斯以秦国文字为基础，参照六国文字，制定出小篆；程邈则根据当时民间流行的、更为简化的字体，整理出隶书。小篆作为秦国标准文字，隶书作为日用文字，两种形体的文字均在全国推广。秦始皇这一"书同文"政策，是中国文字的一次重大改革，对汉字的发展产生了重要影响。

Standardization of the Written Chinese

Before 221 B.C., different states in China during the Spring and Autumn Period and the Warring States Period used different writing system. Even within one state, a character can be written in various ways, which rather hindered nationwide communication. After Qin Shihuang pacified the central plains and unified the six states at 221 B.C., he took a series of measures to manage the country. One of them is to unify the writing system over China.

Under the command of the First Emperor, Li Si the Prime Minister (ca.284 B.C.-208 B.C., a famous politician, writer and calligrapher) and some others began to reform Chinese characters.

● **秦始皇**

秦始皇（前259—前210），政治家、军事家，中国历史上第一个封建王朝的统治者。秦始皇创立皇帝制度，统一了中国，推行"书同文、车同轨"的政策，修筑了万里长城，奠定了中国延续两千多年的基本政治制度。

Qin Shihuang

Qin Shihuang (259 B.C.-210 B.C.) is a prominent statesman, military strategist and ruler of the first feudal state in Chinese history. Qin Shihuang not only unified China, established the imperial system, but took great effort to "standardize the writing script and traffic system", construct the Great Wall and therewith build up the basic political institution for nearly two millennia of imperial rule.

Li Si took the writing system of the State of Qin as basic form and simultaneously referred to Ancient Script of the Six States, finally working out the small seal script. Cheng Miao, however, turned to the simple style popular in the folk, and created the clerical script. Small seal script was introduced nationwide as formal written style, whereas the clerical script was for daily use. This policy has largely reformed Chinese characters and greatly influenced its development.

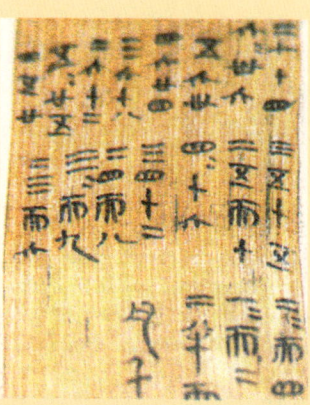

- 木牍（秦）

写有文字的狭长竹、木称为"简"，写有文字的较宽的竹、木称为"牍"。此块秦代木牍上书写的是中国迄今所见最早、最完整的乘法口诀表，字体为秦篆。

Inscribed Wooden Tablet (Qin Dynasty, 221 B.C.-206 B.C.)

The ancient Chinese usually carve words on bamboo or wood. If the inscribed bamboo or wood is long and narrow, they call it slip (*Jian*); if broad, tablet (*Du*). This wooden tablet is engraved with multiplication formula in Qin seal script. It is the earliest and most complete multiplication formula existent in China.

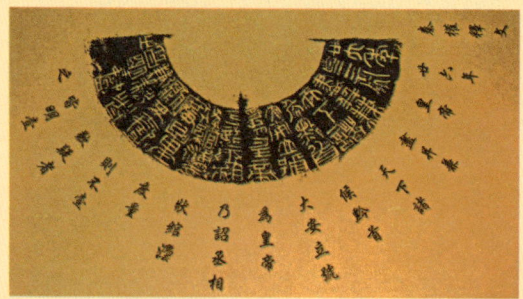

- 《秦始皇诏文铜权》（秦）

铜权，即铜制秤砣。此铜权上的文字为标准的秦篆，书写工整，遒劲有力。诏书大意为：秦始皇帝消灭了所有的诸侯，统一了中国，宣布全国统一度量衡。

Bronze Weight Inscribed with Emperor Qin Shihuang's Decree (Qin Dynasty, 221 B.C.-206 B.C.)

Characters carved in this bronze weight (*Quan*) are standard Qin seal script. It is neatly written, flowing in vigor. The main idea of the imperial edict goes: Emperor Qin Shihuang has wiped out all feudal lords and unified China; now he is to standardize the units of measurement over the nation.

篆更加规范，书写更加简便。隶书分为秦隶和汉隶。起源于战国时期止于秦代的秦隶，是汉字字形和书体演变的一个重要里程碑。汉隶，是西汉使用最广泛的隶书。隶书是由古汉字向现代普遍使用的楷书过渡的字体，为汉字的成熟和稳定奠定了基础。隶书被视为汉字第一个规范化的字体，小篆及其以前的书体被称为"古文字"，即篆书，包括大篆、小篆。大篆即甲骨文、金文、籀文和六国文字，它们保存着古代文字象形的明显特点。隶书及其之后的书体被称为"今文字"。前者更加淳朴、自然，后者则比前者更加成熟、系统。

为了方便书写，在隶书的基础上，出现了草书这一字体。草书，又称"破草"，分为章草、今草、

milestone in the evolution of Chinese characters' writing form. When it came to the Western Han Dynasty (206 B.C.-25 A.D.), clerical script was most widely used. Actually clerical script, as stressed before, is a transitional writing form between ancient Chinese characters and the modern popular regular scripts. It lays the foundation for the maturity of Chinese characters. Besides, clerical script marks the first step of standardization; that is, previous characters like large seal script and small seal script are all "ancient writing forms". Large seal script, including oracle-bone inscription, bronze inscription, *Zhouwen* and Ancient Script of the Six States, maintains the pictographic features of the ancient characters, whereas the clerical script and all later writing forms belong to "the modern category". The former reveals natural simplicity, whereas the latter appears more mature and systematic.

In order to facilitate writing, the cursive script emerged on the basis of the

• 瓦当上的隶书"官"字（汉）
Chinese Character for Official (*Guan*) Written in Clerical Script on the Eave Tile (Han Dynasty, 206B.C.-220A.D.)

狂草。初期的草书称为"章草"，打破了隶书方整、规矩、严谨的局面，是早期草书和汉隶相融的雅化草体，在汉魏之际最为盛行，后至元代（1206—1368）方复兴，蜕变于明代（1368—1644）。汉末，章草进一步"草化"，形成了今草，今草脱去了隶书笔画行迹，上下字之间笔势牵连相通，偏旁出现简化和互借，自魏晋后盛行不

- **钟繇画像**
  钟繇（151—230），字元常，三国时期曹魏著名书法家、政治家，据传是楷书（小楷）的创始人。

  Portrait of Zhong Yao
  Zhong Yao (151-230), style name Yuanchang, is a well-known calligrapher and politician in the State of Wei during the Three Kingdoms Period. He is said to be the father of regular script (also known as small regular script).

clerical script. Cursive script, also referred to as "rough script", can divide into three groups, namely semi-cursive script, regular cursive script and wild cursive script. "Semi-cursive script" is the early form of cursive script. It breaks the strict rules of the regular clerical script and elegantly blends the clerical style of the Western Han Dynasty (206 B.C.-25 A.D.) with the early cursive. This script was quite prevalent during the Han Dynasty and the Wei Dynasty (206 B.C.-280 A.D.), revived in the Yuan Dynasty (1206-1368) yet began to transform in the Ming Dynasty (1368-1644). By the end of the Eastern Han Dynasty, as the semi-cursive script became more scratchy, regular cursive script came into being. Having shaken off all traces of clerical script, the regular cursive script links the succeeding characters in one gesture, simplifies the radical or just shares one with its neighbor. This kind of cursive had been in fashion since the Wei, Western Jin and Eastern Jin dynasties (220-420). Towards the Tang Dynasty (618-907), as the cursive writing became more extravagant, people called it "wild cursive script". Its handwriting stretches and rotates, full of change. But because of its illegibility, people rather appreciate the wild cursive script for

衰。到了唐代（618—907），草书的书写变得更加放纵，因而被称为"狂草"，其笔势连绵环绕，字形奇变百出。但是由于一般人很难认出狂草，所以狂草也就失去了记载、传播信息的文字作用，而变成一种纯艺术性的、仅供欣赏的文字。

魏晋南北朝时期，汉字字体的发展较为错杂，直到楷书的出现才结束这一局面。楷书，又称"真书""正楷"，由隶书逐渐演变而来，因其形体方正，可作楷模，故名。楷书的字形更加简化，将隶书原有的扁平笔画变为方正，省去了汉隶的波势。楷书逐渐取代隶书，成为中国通行的正式字体。楷书的形成，标志着中国文字已经基本定型。三国时期（220—280）的钟繇（151—230）是中国历史上第一个楷书书法家。唐代是楷书发展的鼎盛时期，颜真卿、欧阳询、柳公权等人的楷书作品至今仍备受推崇。到了宋代（960—1279），随着活字印刷术的发展，产生了宋体这一新型字体。

为了书写更加方便，汉字在原有的形体基础上，又演变出了行

its artistic value than use it to record or spread information.

During the Three Kingdoms Period, the Western Jin, Eastern Jin and Northern and Southern dynasties (220-589), the writing forms of Chinese characters were quite intricate. This situation did not end till the emergence of the regular script. Regular script, also known as "true script" or "standard script", derives from the clerical script and is thus named due to its model-like square form. Regular script is much simpler in structure. Unlike the clerical style of the Western Han Dynasty (206 B.C.-25 A.D.), the strokes are rather upright and straight than flat and wavy. Gradually the regular script replaced the clerical script as current official script of China. Indeed, Chinese characters are basically finalized after the formation of regular script. Zhong Yao (151-230) living in the Three Kingdoms Period (220-280) is the first regular script calligrapher in Chinese history. Yet till the Tang Dynasty (618-907) did regular script reach its heyday in development. Masterpieces from famous calligraphers like Yan Zhenqing, Ouyang Xun and Liu Gongquan are still highly regarded today. When it came to the Song Dynasty (960-1279), a new font emerged with the

- 楷书《宣示表》钟繇（三国）

著名的楷书字帖，为三国时的钟繇所书，真迹未传于世，现在所见到的版本为王羲之所临摹。

Memorial of Manifesto to the Throne in Regular Script, by Zhong Yao (Three Kingdoms Period, 220-280)

This famous copybook of regular script is one of Zhong Yao's masterpieces during the Three Kingdoms Period (220-280). But the original version is not handed down from ancient times, so we can only see an imitation from Wang Xizhi (303-361), another remarkable calligrapher in China.

书。行书是楷书的变体，相传为东汉（25—220）刘德升所造。其形体不像楷书那样端正，但是书写比楷书更加流畅、舒展。在汉末，行书未被普遍应用，直至晋朝（265—420）大书法家王羲之书写时，才逐渐兴盛起来。现在，楷书、行书仍被广泛应用于汉字书写。

development of movable-type printing—the Song typeface.

In order to simplify writing, running script gradually evolves from the previous forms of Chinese characters. Running script is a variant of regular script and said to be created by Liu Desheng of the Eastern Han Dynasty (25-220). Unlike regular script, it is not upright in form but writes and extends more smoothly. In the late Eastern Han Dynasty, running script was not in common use. It is until the Jin Dynasty (265-420) when the great calligrapher Wang Xizhi rose to fame, that the running script gradually flourished. Now, both the regular script and the running script are widely used in written Chinese.

In all, the Chinese character is not just a symbol, a tool, but a thick book of

活字印刷术

活字印刷术是中国古代四大发明之一。北宋庆历年间（1041—1048）毕昇发明的泥活字标志了活字印刷的诞生。活字印刷术，是指使用可以移动的金属、胶泥字块进行印刷的方法，比传统的抄写或雕版印刷更加经济。

Movable-type Printing

Movable-type printing is one of the four great inventions of ancient China. Bi Sheng invented clay type during the Qingli Period of the Northern Song Dynasty (1041-1048), which marks the birth of the movable type printing. Movable type is the system of printing and typography that uses movable metals or clay blocks to reproduce documents. It is more economical than traditional transcription and block printing.

• 毕昇画像
Portrait of Bi Sheng (990-1051)

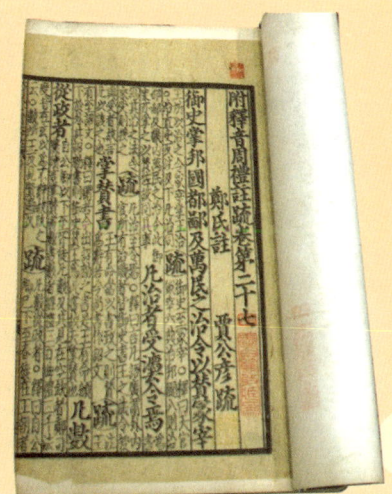

• 刻本《附释音周礼注疏》（宋）
Block-printed *Attached Commentaries on the Rites of Zhou* (Song Dynasty, 960-1279)

汉字不仅仅是一种符号、一种工具，更是一本厚重的历史书，它记载着中国从古至今的文学、思想、民生、经济、自然等各个方面的内容。中国历代皆以汉字为主要官方文字，汉代时，被正式定名为"汉字"。不光在中国，菲律宾、新加坡等国也有一定比例的民众使用汉字，运用汉语交流；中国的邻国日本、韩国，其文字日文、韩文都受到中国汉字的影响，在他们的日常生活中也仍然可以看到汉字。可见中国汉字在世界上的深远影响。

history recording every aspect of society in all ages like literature, thoughts, people's life, economy, nature, etc. Since the beginning, Chinese character has been regarded as the main official language yet not formally named till the Han Dynasty (206 B.C.-220 A.D.). Not only in China, some Philippines and Singaporeans also use Chinese in communication. Besides, Chinese characters also greatly influence languages of the neighbor countries like Japanese and Korean. We can still see Chinese Characters in their daily use. All these reveal the profound impact of Chinese characters in the world.

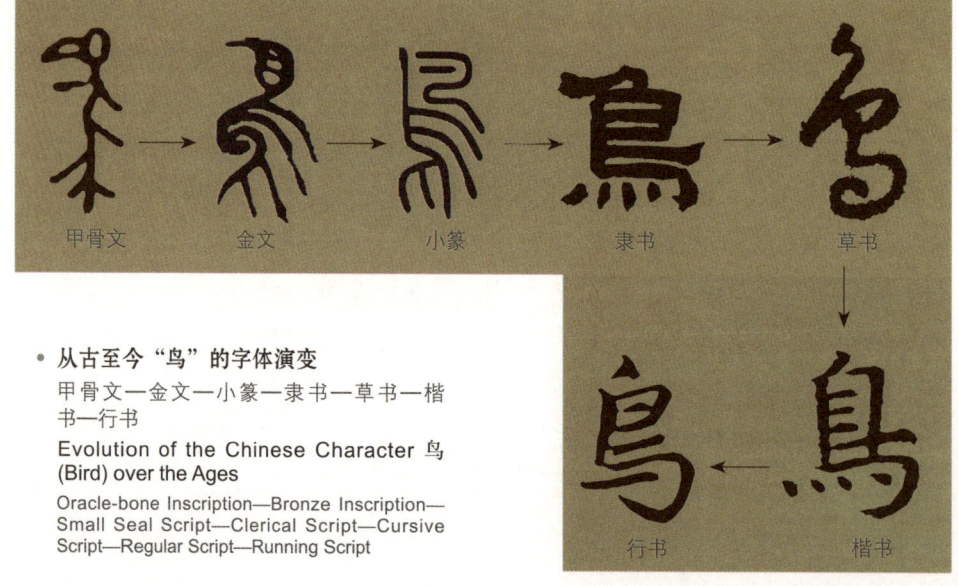

- 从古至今"鸟"的字体演变
  甲骨文—金文—小篆—隶书—草书—楷书—行书
  Evolution of the Chinese Character 鸟 (Bird) over the Ages
  Oracle-bone Inscription—Bronze Inscription—Small Seal Script—Clerical Script—Cursive Script—Regular Script—Running Script

神奇的汉字
The Magical Chinese Characters

　　汉字是一种神奇的文字，集字形、字音、字义三者于一身，具备了发音、独一无二的外形、相应的意义等多方面的内容。掌握一个汉字，要从三方面着手才能够彻底地了解其本质，而这些也是认识汉字、书写汉字、领会汉字的前提条件。

The Chinese character is full of wonder. Each character is three in one, having its own particular form, pronunciation and meaning. To know a character thoroughly, we must examine it from all three aspects. These are indeed prerequisites for a learner who wants to read, write and understand a character.

> 汉字的注音

汉字的标准读音由一个声母、一个韵母和声调确定。汉字有同音不同字的同音字，还有同字不同音的多音字。注音在历史的不同时期一直处于发展变化中，注音方法也有所不同。汉字的注音方法有读若法、直注法、反切法、注音符号以及如今被广泛使用的汉语拼音。

读若法就是用同音或近音的字来给另一个字注音。东汉时期的许慎在其著作《说文解字》中，就是采用读若法给汉字注音的。他写道："埻，射臬也，读若准"，意思是说"埻"字的读音与"准"相同。

直注法就是用一个汉字来标明另一个汉字的读音的注音方法。如"女为说（yuè）已者容"中，使用

> The Phonetic System of Chinese Characters

The standard pronunciation of a Chinese character hinges upon an initial consonant, vowels and a given tone. Like English, Chinese also has homophones as well as polyphones. In different historical periods, phonetic notation has been in development and its methods differ. Generally in its course of development appear altogether five methods of annotation, i.e. *Duruo* Method, *Zhizhu* Method (direct notation), Resection Method (the pronunciation of a character is represented by two other Chinese characters), Phonetic Symbol and the widely used *Hanyu Pinyin*.

Duruo Method, just as the name implies, is to use homophones or characters of similar pronunciation to mark the sound of another character. In the Eastern Han Dynasty (25-220),

- "中国电影"四个字的汉语拼音

"中国电影"四个字的汉语拼音的声调分别为第一声阴平、第二声阳平、第四声去声和第三声上声。

Hanyu Pinyin for the Four Chinese Characters Meaning "Chinese Film"

The tones for "*Zhongguo Dianying*" (Chinese film) are respectively level, rising, falling and falling-rising.

"说者曰悦"来进行注音。

反切法,即用第一个字的声母和第二个字的韵母和声调合拼来注音,这种方法基本可以把所有汉字的发音都组合出来。三国时期（220—280）的经学家孙炎对反切法进行了整理,作《尔雅音义》一

Xu Shen adopted this way of phonetic notation in his work *Shuowen Jiezi* (literally *Explaining and Analyzing Characters*). On one occasion he wrote, "This character means the target for archery, reading like the character meaning permission (*Zhun*)."

The method of direct notation is to use another character to indicate the pronunciation of this character. For instance, in the sentence "A girl will doll herself up for him who pleases her," the speaker borrows another character to indicate "please". In order that people would not read it wrongly, he directly notes that this character reads similar to the character meaning "please".

In the Resection Method, or *Fanqie* Method, the pronunciation of a Chinese character is represented by two other Chinese characters, the first having the same initial consonant as the given character and the second having the same vowels and tone. This method can almost describe all pronunciation of Chinese characters. During the Three Kingdoms Period (220-280), Sun Yan the Confucian scholar further refined this method and wrote a book called *Sounds and Meanings of Erya*. Both *Fan* and *Qie* means combination. About the other two Chinese

书。"反"与"切"同义，是拼合的意思。用作反切的两个字，前一个字叫"反切上字"，简称"上字"，后一个字叫"反切下字"，简称"下字"；被注音的字叫"被反切字"，简称"被切字"。反切的基本原则是上字与被切字的声母相同，下字与被切字的韵母和声调相同，上字的声母、下字的韵母拼合就是被切字的读音。清代的《康熙字典》即采用此方法，例如"毛，莫袍切"。莫的声母是m，袍

characters used in this method, the first is called *Fanqie* upper word, or "upper word" for short; the second is called *Fanqie* lower word, or shortly "lower word". Accordingly, the character to be noted is known as the "*Fanqie*-ed word". The basic rule of this method goes, the upper word has the same initial consonant as the *Fanqie*-ed word, while the lower word has the same vowels and tone, and their combination is the pronunciation of the *Fanqie*-ed word. *Kangxi Dictionary* compiled in the Qing Dynasty (1616-1911) adopted this method of phonetic notation. For instance, to describe the sound of the character *Mao* (hair), the writer borrowed another two characters *Mo* (do not) and *Pao* (gown), then combined the initial consonant of the first character, that is "m", with the vowels of the second character, that is "ao", and finally got the pronunciation for the given character, that is *Mao*. In this example, *Mo* is *Fanqie* upper word, *Pao* is *Fanqie* lower word, and *Mao* is the *Fanqie*-ed word.

Phonetic symbol, still used in Taiwan, is a modern method to describe the pronunciation of a character. It is actually *Pinyin* applied to transcribe an unfamiliar character and can also be used as an input method. A phonetic symbol is made up of initial consonant, vowel and tone. There

• "西单北大街"以汉语拼音注音
Hanyu Pinyin for Xidan North Street

的韵母是ao,两者相合即为毛的音"mao"。其中,莫为反切上字,袍为反切下字,毛为被反切字。

注音符号,是近代中国创造的一种注音工具,至今中国台湾地区仍在使用这种注音方法。注音符号是标注生字的拼音,也可以用做汉字输入法。注音符号由声母、韵母和声调组成。注音符号中有21个声母,16个韵母。注音符号和汉语拼音都能表示汉字的读音,两者可以互相转换。

汉语拼音是中国使用最为广泛的注音方法。汉语拼音采用拉丁字母,由21个声母、39个韵母和五个声调符号、一个隔音符号组成,是一种标注汉字读音的工具,被用来拼写中文。汉语拼音方案是一套表示读音的符号系统,并非字母。首先记住汉语拼音的声母和韵母,再结合不同的音调,就可以拼出汉字的读音。其中,还有许多多音字,这就要结合汉字的字义来判断汉字的读音。五种声调分别是第一声阴平,标为"ˉ";第二声阳平,标为"ˊ";第三声上声,标为"ˇ";第四声去声,标为"ˋ";第五声,轻声,标为"˙"。例如,

are altogether 21 consonants and 16 vowels among the phonetic system. Both the phonetic symbols and *Hanyu Pinyin* can describe the pronunciation of Chinese characters. They are interchangeable in practice.

Pinyin is the most widely used notation method in modern China. It adopts the Latin letters, consists of 21 consonants, 39 vowels, five tones and one syllable-dividing mark and works as a notation tool to help us spell and read Chinese. The Chinese phonetic alphabet is a system of symbols to denote pronunciation, not a group of letters. First you need to remember all the consonants and vowels in the *Pinyin* system, then combine them with different tones, and finally you get the pronunciation of the character. Besides, in Chinese there are many polyphonic characters. Hence sometimes we need to decide the pronunciation of the character by its meaning. With regard to the five tones, the first is termed level tone, labeled " ˉ "; the second is rising tone, labeled " ˊ ", the third is falling-rising tone, labeled " ˇ ", the fourth is falling tone, labeled " ˋ ", the fifth is soft voice, labeled " ˙ ". For example, the character for "China" is spelled as "zhōngguó",

"中国"的拼音为"zhōngguó"，"汉字"的拼音为"hànzì"，"奥运会"的拼音为"àoyùnhuì"。还有一些特殊的情况，比如"西安"的拼音为"xī'ān"，其中'为隔音符号。隔音符号是放在a、o、e前面的特殊符号，它能够使音节的界限清楚，避免产生混淆。如果没有隔音符号，那么西安"(xī'ān)会被念成"先"(xiān)。

"Chinese characters" is spelled as "hànzì", "the Olympic Games" is spelled as "àoyùnhuì". But there are certain special cases. Take the pronunciation of the Chinese city "xi'ān" for instance. The interposed " ' " is a syllable dividing mark usually placed in front of a,o,e, to denote the boundary of syllables and avoid confusion. Without the syllable dividing mark, then the Chinese city "xi'ān" would be read as "xiān" which is another character meaning "before".

《说文解字》

《说文解字》为东汉时期著名的经学家、文字学家、语言学家许慎（约58—约147）所编著，成书于100—121年间。《说文解字》是中国汉字史上第一部按部首编排，分析字形、解说字义、辨识读音的字典，也是唯一一部以汉字为研究对象的经典著作。《说文解字》系统地阐述了汉字的造字规律"六书"，开创了部首检字的先河，现在的汉语字典大多也采用此方法进行检索。

Shuowen Jiezi
(Explaining and Analyzing Characters)

Shuowen Jiezi is compiled from 100 to 121 A.D. by Xu Shen (ca. 58-147), a famous Confucian scholar, philologist and linguist of the Eastern Han Dynasty (25-220). It is the first dictionary in Chinese history that takes characters as its study object. It compiles based on radicals, analyzes the form of the character, explains the meaning and identifies the pronunciation. *Shuowen Jiezi* systematically elaborates upon the formation law, i.e. "the six categories of Chinese characters". It also initiates radical indexing, which now has been used by most Chinese dictionaries.

• 许慎画像
Portrait of Xu Shen

> 汉字的构形

英文是由一个个字母连接起来的，与其不同，汉字由笔画和偏旁等基本单位组合而成。笔画的长短粗细、弯折竖直的不同变化，偏旁的左右上下内外的不同组合，决定了汉字的外形。

- **部与陪**
  "部"与"陪"都是由"阝"和"咅"组成，偏旁的左右位置不同，字形也随之不同，二者的意义也完全不同。
  Chinese Characters *Bu* (Part) and *Pei* (Accompany)
  Both characters are made up of "阝" and "咅", but as the radical "阝" is placed on the right side in the character *Bu*, left in the character *Pei*, they have different shapes and different meanings.

> The Structure of Chinese Characters

Unlike the English word which is a series of letters linked together, the Chinese character is made up of some basic units like strokes and radicals. The length, thickness and variation of the strokes, as well as the different combination of the radicals—left or right, up or down, inside or outside—all determine the shape of the Chinese character.

Strokes of Chinese Characters

Strokes are specific dots and lines, the minimum structural units that form a character. The dot or line created in one motion of the writing brush is called one stroke or one drawing. The sum of strokes or drawings makes up a character. Chinese characters generally consist of eight elemental strokes, respectively

汉字的笔画

汉字的笔画，指构成汉字字形的各种特定的点和线，是汉字的最小结构单位。书写时，起笔到落笔所写的点或线条叫"一笔"或"一画"，汉字就是由这一笔一画构成的。汉字有横、竖、撇、捺、点、提、折、钩八种基本笔画，此外，还有受到字形限制而衍生出来的变形笔画。汉字笔画的组合方式有三种，分别是相交、相接、相离，同

horizontal stroke, vertical stroke, left-falling stroke, right-falling stroke, dot, rising stroke, turning stroke and hook. There are also some variations derived from the particular form of the character. In Chinese, the stroke combination can divide into three categories, intersection, connection and separation. The same set of strokes can construct different characters when using different combinations. Taking the Chinese characters "人" (people) and "八" (eight) for instance, both characters are made up of a left-falling stroke and a right-falling stroke, but in the former, two strokes are connected, whereas in the latter, they are separated.

In order to know the structure of Chinese characters well and avoid wrongly writing, we should be familiar with the strokes and the writing rules.

笔画 Strokes	形状 Shape
点 Dot	、
横 Horizontal Stroke	一
竖 Vertival Stroke	丨
撇 Left-falling Stroke	丿
捺 Right-falling Stroke	㇏
钩 Hook	亅
提 Rising Stroke	㇀
折 Turning Stroke	㇕

• **汉字基本笔画名称表**
除了八种基本笔画之外，还有一些其他的汉字笔画，这些都是汉字的基本结构。
Name-list of the Elemental Strokes of Chinese Character
Apart from the eight elementals, there are some other strokes. All of them are the basic structures of Chinese characters.

样的笔画根据不同的组合方式可以组合成不同的汉字。例如人与八，两个字都是由一撇、一捺构成，一个相接，一个相离。

了解汉字的笔画、知道汉字笔画的书写规则，有利于人们熟悉汉字的结构，避免写错别字。汉字笔画的书写正确与否，还决定了书写的速度和字形的好坏。一般来说，汉字中单体字的笔画较少，合体字的笔画较多。

笔画的书写顺序，叫做"笔顺"。笔顺需要遵循一定的规则，一般情况下为先横后竖，先撇后捺，从上到下，从左到右，先外后内，先外后内再封口，先中间后两边。

汉字笔画的书写运笔也有一定的规律。所有的笔画都是一笔写成，笔画的力度与速度有轻重缓急之分，这是形成书法的重要基础。笔画书写的方法不同，也就形成了不同风格的汉字字形。汉字的书写要根据笔画的形态、大小和位置的不同而有所不同，要做到疏密得当、大小均匀、线条分明、结构稳定，这样才能写出标准的汉字。

Moreover, whether we write the strokes right or not also determines the writing speed and calligraphic quality. In general, the single-component character has less strokes, whereas the compound character has more.

The order of strokes is also known as "the sequence of writing". In writing, we need to follow sequence principles, which, generally speaking, are from the horizontal strokes to the vertical strokes, from the left-falling strokes to the right-falling strokes, from the upper part to the lower part, from the left to the right, from the outer part to the inner part and then seal it with the last stroke, from the middle to the left and the right sides.

In writing, the movement of strokes also goes by certain rules. First, all strokes should be finished within one motion of the brush. Second, the vigor and speed of strokes should have their order of priority. This lays the foundation of calligraphy. By different writing methods, we will get different styles of Chinese characters. Therefore, in order to write standard Chinese characters, we should pay attention to the shape, size and position of the strokes, and achieve proper density, moderate size, clear lines and structural stability.

- 汉字"俊"的笔画解析
  撇竖折点撇点撇折捺
  Strokes of the Chinese Character *Jun* (Pretty)
  They are successively the left-falling stroke, vertical stroke, turning stroke, dot, left-falling stroke, dot, left-falling stroke, turning stroke, and right-falling stroke.

- 汉字"秀"的笔画解析
  撇横竖撇捺折撇
  Strokes of the Chinese Character *Xiu* (Elegant)
  They are successively the left-falling stroke, horizontal stroke, vertical stroke, left-falling stroke, right-falling stroke, turning stroke, and left-falling stroke.

汉字的偏旁

偏旁又叫"部件",是由笔画组成的构成汉字的基本单位。位于字左边的偏旁叫"左偏旁";位于字右边的偏旁叫"右偏旁"。一般情况下,汉字由形旁和声旁组成,形旁表示汉字的字形,声旁表示汉字的字音。汉字包括独体字和合体字,独体字不能分割,由笔画构

Radicals of Chinese Characters

Radical, also known as "component", is the basic unit of Chinese characters which is made up of strokes. "Left radical", as the name suggests, is radical placed on the left side of the character, while "right radical" is placed on the right side. In most cases, a Chinese character is made up of a pictographic part and a phonetic part: the former denotes the configuration of the character, the latter suggests the

成；合体字可以分割，由独体字、偏旁、部首（按照汉字字形结构，取其相同部位，作为查字依据，其相同部位，称为"部首"）和其他不成字的部件等基础部件组合构成。在合体字中，无论是其上下、左右还是内外，任何一个结构单位都可以统称为"偏旁"。偏旁的常见组合方式有：上下结构、左右结构、上中下结构、左中右结构、半包围结构、全包围结构、"品"字形结构，等等。

很多汉字在作为偏旁出现时，会出现一定的变形，例如"水"字作偏

- **田字格中的"和"字**
  田字格是外形像"田"字的格子，"和"字的笔画在相应的区间里。
  Chinese Character for "Harmony" (*He*) Written on Field-lined Practice Paper
  The practice paper is a framework of crisscrossed lines, and the Chinese character for "harmony" is written within the grid.

pronunciation. Chinese characters can be divided into single-components and compounds. The single-component is made up of strokes and cannot be further divided. The compound, however, can be divided and is constructed by single-component, radical (a radical is the same structural element shared by a group of characters and commonly used as index in Chinese dictionary) and other non-character components. In the compound, any structural unit can be referred to as "radical", no matter it is in the upper or lower part, right or left side, inner or outer part of the character. The common combination modes for radicals include top-bottom structure, left-right structure, top-middle-bottom structure, left-middle-right structure, half-enclosed structure, enclosed structure and " 品 "-shaped (or triple-lapped) structure.

Many Chinese Characters will somehow be deformed when used as radicals. For instance, when the Chinese character for "water" (*Shui*) serves as a radical, it is written as " 氵 " like three drops of water. Likewise, the word for "hand" (*Shou*) is changed into " 扌 " yet still like an erect hand.

Because of their different positions, the radicals can form various compound

半包围结构的汉字"匿"，匚（三匡儿）旁
Chinese Character for "Hide" (*Ni*) in Half-enclosed Structure with Radical of "匚"

全包围结构的汉字"围"，囗（方匡儿）旁
Chinese Character for "Surround" (*Wei*) in Enclosed Structure with Radical of "囗" like Square Frame

品字形结构的汉字"品"
Chinese Character for "Product" or "Taste" (*Pin*) in Triple-lapped Structure

032
汉字
Chinese Characters

匿 围 品
蟹 葱 捕 狱

上下结构的汉字"蟹"，虫字旁
Chinese Character for "Crab" (*Xie*) in Top-Bottom Structure with Radical of "虫" Meaning Worm

左右结构的"捕"，扌（提手）旁
Chinese Character for "Catch" (*Bu*) in Left-Right Structure with Radical of "扌" Meaning Erect Hand

上中下结构的"葱"，艹（草字头）旁
Chinese Character for "Green Onion" (*Cong*) in Top-Middle-Bottom Structure with Radical of "艹" Meaning Grass

左中右结构的"狱"，犭（反犬）旁
Chinese Character for "Prison" (*Yu*) in Left-Middle-Right Structure with Radical of "犭" Related to Animals

• 不同结构的汉字
  Different Structures of Chinese Characters

旁时写做"氵"，"手"字作偏旁时写做"扌"。

组成合体字的偏旁因其位置不同，可以组合成不同的字。通过一个汉字谜语就可以很好地理解："一木口中栽，非困又非呆，若是把杏念，趁早别来猜。"谜底是"约束"的"束"字。

characters. To understand this phenomenon better, we may first try to solve the riddle below. "A tree（木）is planted in the square frame（口）, but it is not the characters for sleepy（困）or stupid（呆）. Do you think it is the word for apricot（杏）? No, just try again." The answer is the Chinese character "束" meaning constraint.

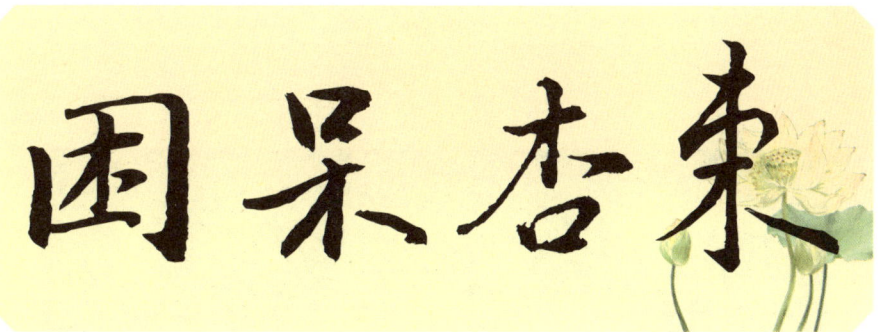

- 汉字"困" "呆" "杏" "束"
  四个字均为"口"旁和"木"旁的组合。
  The Chinese Character for "Sleepy" (*Kun*), "Stupid" (*Dai*), "Apricot" (*Xing*) and "Constraint" (*Shu*)
  They are all a combinatren of the radical "口"and "木".

谜语

　　谜语，源自中国古代民间，由隐语（隐意的语言）发展而来，是古代人集体智慧的结晶。谜语主要指暗射事物、文字等供人猜测的隐语，或者引申为蕴含深奥意义的事物。谜语分为事物谜和文义谜两大类，事物谜主要猜测常见的事物，例如玩具、动植物、建筑等；文义谜主要猜测单字、词语、词组、短句等。在古代民间，流传着元宵佳节猜灯谜的文字游戏。灯谜，即挂在纱灯上的谜语。

Riddle

Riddles originate from the Chinese folk. They evolve from the hidden meaning of Chinese language and crystallize the collective wisdom of the ancient people. A riddle mainly alludes to an object or character or implies a thing of profound meaning by signs, then leaving others to guess. Hence riddles can generally divide into two groups: one is for common things, like toy, plant, animal, building, etc.; the other is related to literary writing, like a single character, expression, phrase, short sentence, etc. Among the ancient folk, word games were quite popular during the Lantern Festival. They are just riddles hanging on the gauze-wrapped lanterns.

• 灯谜长廊（图片提供：全景正片）
Gallery of Lanterns Written with Riddles

> 汉字的字义

　　汉字是集字形、字音、字义三者于一体的文字系统，字形、字音与字义密不可分。汉字的字形记录着字义，同时字义又影响着字音。中国早期汉字如甲骨文、金文，其图画意味很明显，可以"望形知义"，而现在的汉字则很少能够通过字形直接知道汉字的字义。

　　汉字是表意文字，在先人创造文字的时候，其形体一般都能说明其具体或者类别意义。通过汉字的字形，来分析汉字的来源与演变而获得汉字的字义，这种方法叫做"造字分析法"，又叫做"字源分析法"。汉字有许多多音字、同音字和近音字，了解汉字的字义可以避免使用错别字。

　　例如，"贝"与"北"是一对

> The Semantic Meaning of Chinese Characters

In Chinese, the graphic form, pronunciation and semantic meaning are closely connected and all integrated in one character. As the graphic form bears the semantic meaning of the character, the semantic meaning also affects the pronunciation. Early Chinese characters, like the oracle-bone inscriptions and bronze inscriptions are quite picturesque. Simply from the appearance can we guess their meaning. In contrast, modern Chinese characters are more abstract. It is rarely possible to see the meaning directly from the graphic form.

　　Chinese characters are pictograms. That is, when our ancestors first created the written Chinese, we can generally recognize its specific or category meaning from the form. This method, to get the semantic meaning of the character by

近音字，但是两者所表示的意思却大相径庭。"北"在古文字中的本义是相背、相反的意思；现在，北代表方位，与南相对。"贝"在古文字中的本义是海贝，是古代的货币，因此现在以贝为偏旁的汉字大多和钱财有关。从这两个字的甲骨文字形上，就可以分析出"北"与"贝"的字源发展，从而知道两者的意义。

analyzing its origin and evolution through its graphic form, is called "analysis method of character creation" or "analysis method of etymology". There are many polyphones, homophones and near-sound characters in Chinese. A knowledge of the semantic meaning can help us avoid using the characters wrongly.

For instance, the Chinese characters for "shell" (bèi) and "north" (běi) are similar in articulation but widely divergent in semantic meaning. In ancient Chinese text, the latter means "contrary", but now it is the antonym of "south", indicating direction. The former originally means seashell, which serves as ancient currency, so now most Chinese characters related to money have the character for "shell" (bèi) as radical. From the oracle-bone inscriptions of

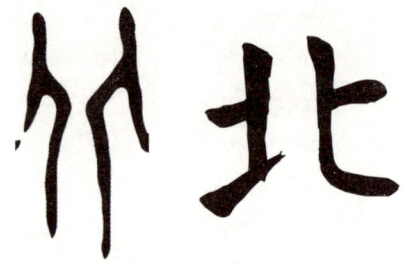

• 甲骨文、楷体的"北"
The Chinese Character for "North" (*Bei*) in oroule-bone Inscriptions and Regular Script

• 甲骨文、楷体的"贝"
The Chinese Character for "Shell" (*Bei*) in Oracle-bone Inscription and Regular Script

汉字中的形声字完美地体现了字音、字形与字义之间的关联,一般来说,声旁表示字音,形旁表示字义。许多汉字的偏旁具有表意的功能,有的形旁可以完全表意,例如,父字旁的"爸",光字旁的"辉"。父,在甲骨文中的字形很像是一个人手持石斧,本义为从事劳动的男人,后来"父"常常指代父亲,也是对与父母同辈份的长辈的尊称。"爸","父"字旁,同"父",父亲的意思。甲骨文中的"光",上方是两个点,代表火光,下方是一个跪着的人形,组合在一起表示人的头顶上有火光,象

these two characters, we can explore the etymology of shell (bèi) and north (běi), and then decipher their meanings.

In Chinese, the pictophonetic characters perfectly illustrate the relation between the phonetic pronunciation, graphic form and semantic meaning. Generally speaking, the phonetic part suggests the pronunciation of the character, while the pictographic part suggests the meaning. In many cases, a radical can demonstrate the meaning of the character, and sometimes the pictographic part is completely ideographic. For example, the Chinese character for "father" (Ba) has Fu as radical which also means father. The

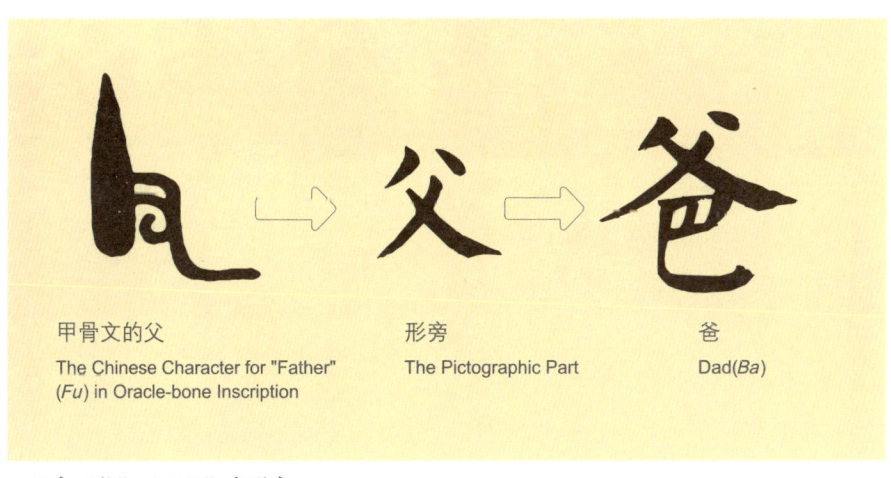

甲骨文的父
The Chinese Character for "Father" (Fu) in Oracle-bone Inscription

形旁
The Pictographic Part

爸
Dad(Ba)

- 汉字"爸"以"父"为形旁
  Chinese Character for "Dad" with "the Father" as the Pictographic Part

甲骨文的光
The Chinese Character for "Light" (*Guang*) in Oracle-bone Inscription

形旁
The Pictographic Part

辉
Glory (*Hui*)

- 汉字"辉"以"光"为形旁
  Chinese Character for "Glory" with "Light" as the Pictographic Part

征着明亮。"辉",右侧为"光"字,光辉的意思。

有的形旁可以表示字义的大致类别,例如,鸟字旁的"鹊",木字旁的"松"。甲骨文中的"鸟"就是鸟的形状,本义是飞禽的总称。鹊,由"昔""鸟"两个偏旁组成,本义为喜鹊,是一种鸟类。木,本义是树木,甲骨文中的"木"就是树木的形状。松,其偏旁为木,松树的简称,是一种常绿乔木。

有的形旁与字义直接相关,例如火字旁的"烧",土字旁的"地"。火,在甲骨文中是一团火焰的轮廓,本义指物体燃烧所发出

radical of the Chinese character for "glory" (*Hui*) is *Guang* which also means light. In oracle-bone inscription, the character *Fu* looks quite like a person with stone axes in hands, so it is originally used to indicate laboring man, and then gradually becomes a synonym for father, or a respectful term to address elders like our parents. Hence the character *Ba* (father) has the character *Fu* as radical. In oracle-bone inscription, the character *Guang* has two dots above representative of firelight, and a man kneeling below. Such a combination symbolizes brightness, so the character *Hui* (glory) has *Guang* as radical.

Some pictographic part can show the category meaning of the character. For

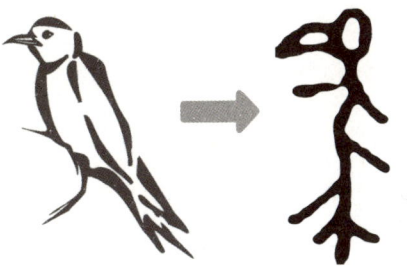

- 甲骨文"鸟"
  The Chinese Character for "Bird" (*Niao*) in Oracle-bone Inscription

- 鹊
  The Chinese Character for "Magpie" (*Xique*)

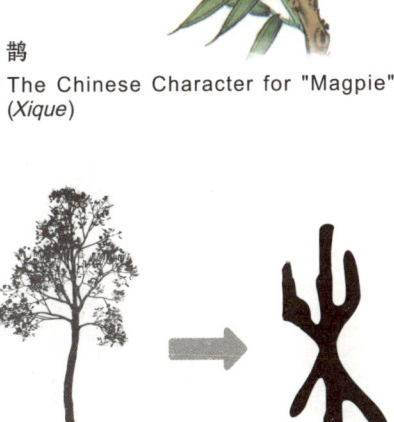

- 甲骨文"木"
  The Chinese Character for "Wood" (*Mu*) in Oracle-bone Inscription

example, the radical of *Que* (magpie) is *Niao* (bird), the radical of *Song* (pine) is *Mu* (wood). In oracle-bone inscription, the written form of *Niao* is similar to the shape of a bird; it is the general term for all feathered flying animals. The character *Que* is made up of two radicals, *Xi* (past) and *Niao* (bird), from which we can see it refers to a kind of bird, magpie, to be specific. *Mu* originally means tree and appears just like a tree in oracle-bone inscription. The character *Song* has *Mu* as radical, indicating the evergreen pine tree, or pine for short.

Some pictographic part is directly related with the meaning of the character, such as the character *Shao* (burning) which has *Huo* (fire) as radical, or the character *Di* (land) which has *Tu* (earth)

- 松
  The Chinese Character for Pine Tree (*Song*)

甲骨文"火"
The Chinese Character for "Fire" (*Huo*) in Oracle-bone Inscription

燃烧
The Chinese Expression for "Burning" (*Ranshao*)

- 甲骨文"土"
The Chinese Character for "Earth" (*Tu*) in Oracle-bone Inscription

- 土地
The Chinese Character for "Land" (*Tudi*)

的光、火焰和热。"烧",火字旁,本义是使物体着火。想要让物体燃烧,就必须有火,烧与火直接相关。"土",在甲骨文中是地面上的一个土堆,其本义为泥土、土壤。"地",土字旁,本义为大地,大地是由土壤、泥土等组成的,与土息息相关。

as radical. In Oracle-bone inscription, *Huo* is the contour of agitated flames and originally means light, flame and heat emitted by a burning object. The character *Shao* means "to burn", having *Huo* (fire) as radical. We need fire to burn an object, so we can see *Shao* and *Huo* are directly connected. The character *Tu* in the oracle-bone inscription appears like a mound on the ground and originally means soil or earth. *Di* has *Tu* (earth) as radical, meaning land. The land is composed of soil and earth, so *Tu* and *Di* are closely related with each other.

> 汉字造字法

中华民族的先民经过长期的积累，创造了丰富而博大精深的汉字体系。经过几千年的发展演变，汉字仍旧被中华民族所使用，其总量最多时有近十万字，日常使用的汉字也有几千字。先民通过日常积累，运用六书造字法创造了各式各样的汉字。

六书造字法，指象形、指事、会意、形声、转注和假借六种造字方法。"六书"一词最早出现在西周时期的儒家经典著作《周礼》一书中，但没有加以解释。东汉时期，许慎的《说文解字》一书详细地阐释了六书的含义，这也是历史上对六书定义的首次正式记载。

> The Formation of Chinese Characters

After years of accumulation, Chinese ancestors finally gave birth to the colorful and profound Chinese characters system. After thousands of years of evolution, the Chinese characters are still in use. Moreover, its number once reached a hundred thousand in total, among which thousands are for everyday use. Thus day in and day out, by the Six Categories of Chinese Characters the ancients brought into being all kinds of Chinese characters.

The Six Categories of Chinese Characters include six formation laws, namely pictographic character, self-explanatory character, associative compound character, pictophonetic character, mutually explanatory character and phonetic loan character. The term first appeared in *Rites of Zhou*, one of the Confucian classics during the

象形

象形造字法，就是依照事物的外貌特征，用线条、笔画描绘出来的造字方法。用象形造字法创造的

Western Zhou Dynasty (1046 B.C.-771 B.C.), but it gives no further explanation, though mentioned. Until the Eastern Han Dynasty (25-220), did Xu Shen detailedly elaborate upon the

- 甲骨文"虎"

虎，即老虎。从其甲骨文的字形上看，尖牙、利爪、斑纹都栩栩如生，极像一只跃起捕杀猎物的猛虎。中国古人认为"虎"是趋吉避凶的瑞兽，其在中国文化中有着丰富的意义。

The Chinese Character for "Tiger" (*Hu*) in Oracle-bone Inscription
From the oracle-bone inscription of the character, we can see fangs, claws and stripes, all so vivid, presenting a fierce tiger leaping to pray. For the ancient Chinese, tiger is an auspicious animal able to bring good fortune and avoid disaster, so it assumes many meanings in Chinese culture.

- 老虎
Tiger

• 甲骨文"麦"

麦，即麦子。从其甲骨文的字形上看为一棵麦子，从上到下分别为麦穗、叶子和根部。麦，是一种草本植物，包括小麦、大麦、燕麦以及黑麦等品种，是人们熟悉的粮食作物。

The Chinese Character for "Cereal Grass" (*Mai*) in Oracle-bone Inscription

In oracle-bone inscription, the character for cereal grass looks just like a wheat in form, with ears, leaves and roots from top to bottom. Cereal grass is a herb of the genus Triticum, including such food crops as wheat, barley, oat, rye and other varieties. It is one of the most common crops for Chinese.

• 小麦（图片提供：全景正片）
Wheat

文字叫做"象形字",象形字来源于图画,因此较为容易辨认和区别。汉字中的动物、器物等,这些在实际生活中出现的实物,大多为象形字,它们都具有形象的外貌特征。

指事

随着人们沟通、交流的语言不断丰富,指事、会意、形声等造字

meaning of the Six Categories of Chinese Characters in *Shuowen Jiezi*. This is also its first official definition historically documented.

Pictographic Character

Pictographic character is a hieroglyph that describes the physical characteristics of the object by means of lines or strokes. Characters thus formed are known as "pictographic character". As this kind of

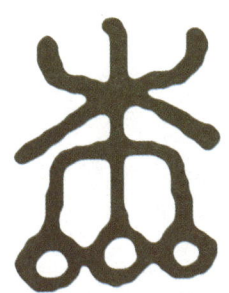

- 金文"本"

本,指代树木的根部,从其金文的字形上看,形似树木的根须。"末"意为树梢,与"本"相对应,现在的"本"引申意为事物的源头和根本,有成语"本末倒置",比喻把主次、轻重的位置弄颠倒了。

The Chinese Character *Ben* in Bronze Inscription

Ben originally refers to the root of the tree and in bronze inscription, the character looks quite like real roots. Now people often use its extended sense, indicating origin and foundation. *Mo* is opposite to *Ben*, meaning treetop. In one Chinese idiom, people say "put *Mo* before *Ben*," which corresponds to the English proverb "put the cart before the horse," both signifying one reverses the order of importance.

- 树木的根部
Tree Roots

- **甲骨文"申"**

申，本义是雷电闪光的样子，从其甲骨文的字形上看，很像下雨天雷电所发出的光束。现在，申有陈述、说明的意思，例如申诉、申辩等。

The Chinese Character *Shen* in Oracle-bone Inscription

Shen, originally used to describe the flash of lightening on the rainy day, much resembles the thunder beam in oracle-bone inscription. Now the character also means to state, explain, plead, argue, etc.

雷电（图片提供：全景正片）
Thunder and Lightning

方法逐渐出现，它们在原有的象形字基础上，通过对象征性符号进行拼合、增减而形成新的文字。指事造字法，就是用象征性的符号或在图形上加些指示性符号，来表示文字意义的造字方法。使用指事造字法创造的文字叫做"指事字"。在象形字的基础上，指事字增加了表意的标志，它是会意字、形声字的重要构成要素。指事字表达的一般是抽象概念，文字意义更加隐晦，指事字的数量是六种造字法所创造的汉字中最少的。

会意

会意造字法是根据汉字的意义关系，将两个或两个以上的字组合

character is quite pictorial in appearance, they are relatively easy to identify and distinguish. Most characters related to animals, utensils or other substantial objects in real life are pictographs, all retaining the physical characteristics of the signified.

Self-explanatory Character

As the language people used in communication became richer, other character formation laws gradually appeared, like the self-explanatory character, associative compound character, pictophonetic character, etc. These new characters are created on the basis of previous pictograms and then compound, increase or decrease the symbols. One method is to represent meaning by using symbols or adding indicative marks to the existing graphic character. Characters thus coined are

- 金文"嵩"

嵩，本义是山高，从其金文的字形上看，上半部分是"山"的形状，下半部分是一个"高"字。现在，嵩专指地名，例如五岳之中的嵩山。

The Chinese Character *Song* in Bronze Inscription

Song is originally used to describe the height of mountains. From its bronze inscription, we can see the upper part of the character is mountain-shaped, while the latter part is another Chinese character *Gao* meaning high. Now the character Song is a toponym, referring specifically to Songshan, one of the Five Sacred Mountains in China.

成一个字的造字方法。用会意造字法创造的文字叫做"会意字"。例如，"明"由"日"和"月"组成，其意义是指日光加月光，即光明。还有两个或者几个同样的字重叠而成的会意字，例如两个"木"组成的"林"，意为树林；两个"人"组成的"从"，意为跟从、跟随；三个"木"组成的"森"，意为森林；三个"人"组成的"众"，意为众多。

generally called "self-explanatory character". Indeed, the self-explanatory character usually has ideographic signs added to the pictogram to denote meaning. It also constitutes one important element of the associative compound character and pictophonetic characters. But as self-explanatory characters usually convey abstract ideas and obscure literal meaning, its number is the least among all the Six Categories of Chinese Characters.

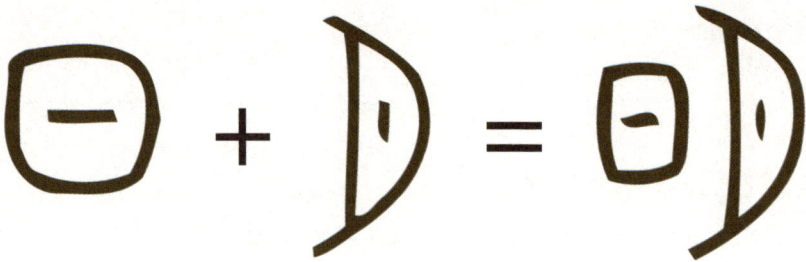

- "日""月"结合即光明

Ri (sun) and *Yue* (moon) Make up Brightness

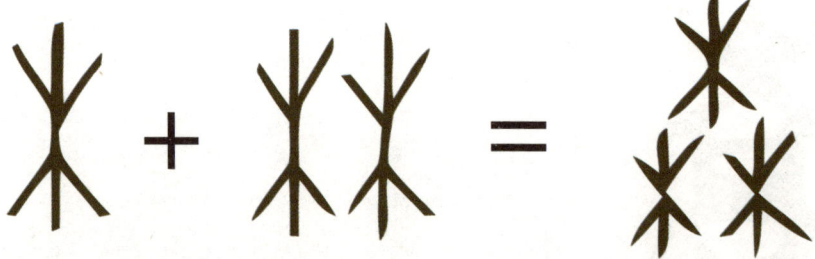

- "木""林"结合即森林

Mu (wood) and *Lin* (forest) Make up Forest

形声

形声造字法，是指由形旁和声旁共同组成文字的一种造字法，形旁代表文字的意义，声旁表示文字的发音。因为汉字是表意性的文字，不能直接显示字音，除了需要依靠拼音来注明字音外，声旁也可

- 小篆"蝶"

"蝶"是左形右声的形声字，本义为蝴蝶。从其小篆的字形上看，左侧是"虫"的形状，说明蝶属于昆虫；右边为枼（yè），是"葉"字的本字，表示字音。

The Chinese Character for "Butterfly" (*Die*) in Small Seal Script

Die meaning butterfly is a pictophonetic character, with the pictographic part on the left side of the phonetic. From the small seal script, we can see the left part of the character appears worm-like, implying that butterfly is a kind of insect. The right part is another character *Ye* (leaf), which on the one hand denotes pronunciation of the compound.

Associative Compound Character

Associative compound character combines two or more characters of related meaning to create a third one. Character thus coined is also known as ideogrammic compound character. For instance, combining *Ri* (sun) and *Yue* (moon), the two natural sources of light, makes *Ming* (bright). Sometimes, to double or triple a character can also produce an associative compound character. For example, doubling the pictogram *Mu* (tree) produces *Lin* (grove), while tripling it produces *Sen* (forest). Similarly, doubling the character *Ren* (man) produces *Cong* (follower), while tripling it produces *Zhong* (multitude).

- 蝴蝶
  Butterfly

- 小篆"菜"

"菜"是一个上形下声的形声字，本义为蔬菜。小篆中，其字形很像是草，说明菜属于草本植物，下边的"采"，表示字音。

The Chinese Character for "Vegetable" (*Cai*) in Small Seal Script

Cai meaning vegetable is another pictophonetic character with the pictographic part stacked on top of the phonetic. In small seal script, the character looks much like grass, which illustrates it is a kind of herb. The character *Cai* (pick) in the lower part denotes the pronunciation of the compound.

以帮助提供字音信息。用形声造字法创造的文字叫做"形声字"。形声是汉字造字法中造字最多的方法，形声字占汉字总数的80%以上。受到古今字音、字形变化的影响，现在的形声字声旁的表音作用已经十分有限。

形声字的形旁和声旁有六种组合方式：左形右声，左声右形，上形下声，上声下形，内形外声，内声外形。

转注

转注造字法，是指两个字互相注释，用转注造字法创造的文字叫做"转注字"。转注造字法有三种不同的说法，一是形同而转，二是

Pictophonetic Character

This kind of character is made up of a pictographic part and a phonetic part. The former suggests the meaning of the character, while the latter denotes its pronunciation. As Chinese characters are ideographic and hence cannot directly show the pronunciation, we need both the *Pinyin* system for phonetic notation and the phonetic part to provide pictophonetic character. Characters thus coined are collectively called pictophonetic characters. The majority of Chinese characters—above 80%—are formed in this way. But owing to the changes of sound and the simplification of the written form in modern times, the phonetic part of many characters no longer accurately represents their pronunciation.

- 甲骨文"考"

考，本义为年老，本身为象形字，与"老"字互相转注。从其甲骨文的字形上看，像一位头发稀疏的驼背老人拄着拐杖慢慢行走着。现在，"考"依旧有年老的含义，词语"寿考"，意为寿命长。

The Chinese Character for "Test" (*Kao*) in Oracle-bone Inscription

Kao, originally meaning old is a pictograph synonymous to the character *Lao* (old). In oracle-bone inscription, the form of *Kao* looks just like a thin-haired and hunchbacked old man walking slowly with a cane. Now, the character retains the meaning "old". There is also a related term *Shoukao*, meaning longevity.

义同而转，三是音同而转。由转注造字法所创造的文字字数较少。

假借

假借造字法，就是借用现有的一个与其同音或音近的字来表达这个本不存在的字。用假借造字法产生的文字叫做"假借字"，它与本有其字、但和另一个字通用的通假字不同。

People usually combine the pictographic part and the phonetic part in six modes: a. the pictographic part is on the left side of the phonetic part, or vice versa; b. the pictographic part is stacked on the top of the phonetic part, or vice versa; c. the pictographic part may be placed inside the phonetic part, or vice versa.

Mutually Explanatory Character

Characters coined in this way can mutually explain each other. They may be similar in form but diverged in meaning and pronunciation, or similar in meaning, diverged in pronunciation and form, or similar in pronunciation but diverged in form and meaning. Mutually explanatory character only occupy a small proportion in Chinese characters.

Phonetic Loan Character

This category covers cases where an existing character is used to represent a nonexistent word with similar or identical pronunciation. The phonetic loan character, also known as loaned or borrowed character, is different from the "*Tongjia* character", which is an interchangeable character used for an existing homophonous character.

- 甲骨文"采"

  采，本义为用手指轻轻摘取，它是"採"的本字。从其甲骨文的字形上看，就像是一只手正在采摘树上的果实。

  The Chinese Character for "Pick" (*Cai*) in Oracle-bone Inscription

  Cai (采) meaning "pick gently with your hands", is the original form of the character *Cai* (採). In oracle-bone inscription, the latter character looks just like a hand picking fruit on the tree.

- 金文"辰"

  辰，本义是用蛤蚌壳磨制成的农具，是"蜃"的本字。从其金文的字形上看，好像是蛤蚌之类的软体动物。

  The Character for "Celestial Bodies" (*Chen*) in Bronze Inscription

  Chen (辰) originally refers to farm tools made of clam shells and is the original form of the character *Shen* (蜃) meaning clam. In bronze inscription, the character quite resembles the clam or other kinds of mollusk in appearance.

通假字

通假字是中国古书的用字现象之一。因为一些原因，书写时没有使用本字，而临时借用了音同或音近的字来替代。有人认为部分通假字就是古人所写的白字。例如，"女"通"汝"。读音为rǔ，意思是"你"。

Tongjia Character

The *Tongjia* or interchangeable character often appears in the ancient Chinese texts. For some reasons, the writer did not use the original word, but temporarily borrowed another character of identical or similar pronunciation to substitute. Some would believe that *Tongjia* characters are simply those misused by the ancients. For example, the character for "you" (rǔ) is replaced by the character for "woman" (nǚ).

优美的汉字
The Graceful Chinese Characters

　　汉字的外形方方正正，这一特点使其很容易与世界上其他国家、民族和地区的文字区别开。汉字的字形丰富多样，充满了节奏韵律，还可以通过书法、篆刻、诗词及对联等艺术形式，向大众彰显其独特魅力。

As Chinese characters all appear square in shape, it is easier to distinguish them from the language of other countries, peoples and regions in the world. Indeed, as the written Chinese is rich, varied and full of rhythm, which emits its unique charm through all kinds of art forms like calligraphy, seal carving, poetry, couplets, etc.

> 汉字与书法

汉字的美最为突出地表现在其外形：或俊秀飘逸、或雄劲沉稳的线条，或疏密相间、或紧凑别致的布局。所谓"书画同源"，指汉字的起源与图画密切相关，汉字向书法艺术的发展可谓有迹可循。书法，是汉字、蒙古文、阿拉伯文等世界上少数几种文字的艺术表现形

> Chinese Characters and Calligraphy

The beauty of Chinese characters most prominently shows in its written form, or specifically in the elegant or vigorous lines, and the well-balanced or close-knitted layout. As the old saying goes, "Calligraphy and painting share the same origin." The origin of Chinese characters is indeed closely related to

- 优美的中国扇

  清代吴昌硕的桃花扇、陆廉夫的设色山水扇，将书法与绘画相结合，呈现出一种不一样的美感。

  The Graceful Chinese Fans
  The peach blossoms on the fan are painted by Wu Changshuo (1844-1927) of the Qing Dynasty, while the landscape is colored by Lu Lianfu (1851-1920). The winning combination of calligraphy and painting reveals a unique aesthetic perception.

中国扇

扇子是夏季必备的引风纳凉工具,最早称为"翣(shà)",距今已有3000多年的历史。起初,扇子是一种礼仪工具,作为地位与权力的象征,在漫长的发展过程中才逐渐演变成具有独特美感的实用工具。中国的扇文化有着深厚的文化底蕴,是中华传统文化的重要组成部分。中国扇从长柄的雉扇、真丝的绢扇、羽毛制作的羽扇到今日常见的折扇,逐渐发展成为集书法、绘画、刺绣、编织等艺术为一体的文化产品。

Chinese Fans

Fan is an indispensable hand-held instrument used in summer to cool oneself by airflows. It is originally known as *Sha* and has a history of more than 3,000 years. At the beginning, fans were only ceremonial tools symbolic of one's social status and power. Only after a long time of development, did they gradually become practical tools with unique beauty. The Chinese fan has a rich cultural heritage and constitutes an important part of the national culture. From the long-

- **折扇**
  折扇源于南北朝(420—589),以竹木做扇骨,韧纸做扇面,扇面上还可题诗作画。
  Folded Fan
  The folded fan first appeared in the Northern and Southern dynasties (420-589). The fan bone is made of bamboo. The fan screen is made of tough paper and adorned with poem and painting.

handled pheasant tail fan, to the silk fan, feathered fan and modern folded fan, we can see the development of the fan culture, which progressively integrates calligraphy, painting, embroidery, waving and other artistic techniques into one.

- 羽扇
  羽扇是最早出现的扇子，距今已有2000多年历史。
  Feathered Fan
  Feathered fan is the earliest fan ever existent with a history of more than 2,000 years.

- 团扇
  团扇，也叫"宫扇""纨扇"，是一种圆形有柄的扇子。
  Round Fan
  Round fan, also known as "palace fan" or "white silk fan", is round, handled.

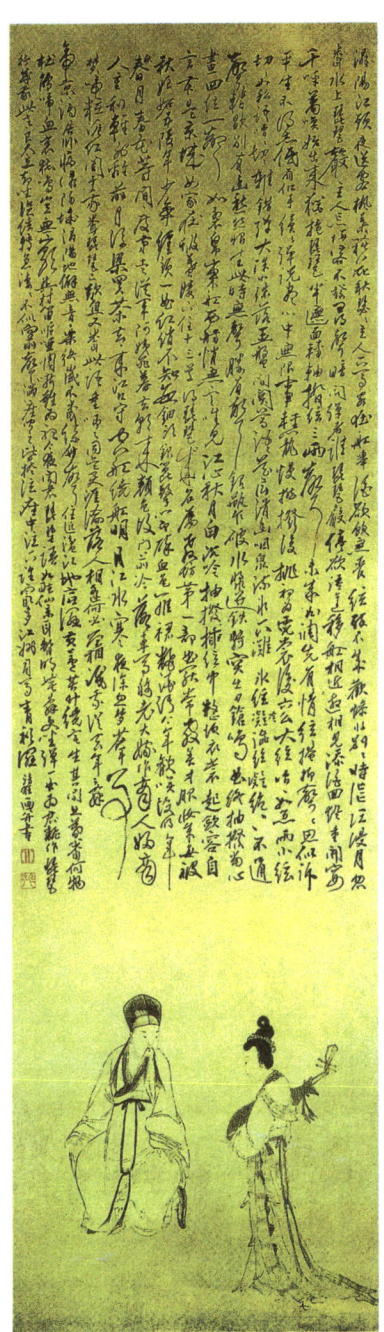

- 《琵琶行图》（明）

《琵琶行》是唐代著名诗人白居易(772—846)的一首诗歌代表作，形象地描绘了歌女演奏琵琶的情景。此图为明代画家郭诩（1456—1532）所作，描绘了白居易与演奏《琵琶行》的歌女邂逅的情景。占画面2/3篇幅的《琵琶行》诗为行草体书写，纵横奔放。

Painting of Song of the Pipa Player (Ming Dynasty, 1368-1644)

Song of the Pipa Player is a masterpiece by Bai Juyi (772-846), a famous poet in the Tang Dynasty (618-907). The poem vividly depicts a female playing *Pipa*. This scroll is painted by Guo Xu (1456-1532) of the Ming Dynasty, showing the poet's encounter with the performer who is playing the *Song of the Pipa Player*. Written in unrestrained semi-cursive style, the poem occupies about two-thirds of the whole picture.

drawing, which hence enables us to track the development of calligraphy. Calligraphy is an art of fine handwriting only shared by a few written languages in the world like Chinese characters, Mongolian and Arabic. The Chinese calligraphy is a traditional art unique to Chinese characters. It is highly honored as "wordless poetry, lineless dancing, imageless painting, and soundless music."

The calligraphy is almost ubiquitous, casting its shadow over all kinds of practical or artistic works such as Chinese paintings, Chinese fans, couplets written on columns of the hall, horizontal inscribed boards, buildings, paper-cuts, etc. Actually, the beautiful Chinese

- 山西王家大院"凝瑞"门匾

门匾是横挂在建筑物门屏上的装饰，用来表达义理、感情。王家大院是典型的山西富商民居，门匾上的"凝瑞"两字意为聚集祥瑞。

Board Inscribed with *Ningrui* (Gather Auspice) on the Door Lintel of Wang's Grand Courtyard at Shanxi Province

The inscribed board is a common decoration horizontally hung upon the door lintel of the building to express moral principles or feelings. The Wang's Grand Courtyard is a typical house of this kind built by a wealthy merchant of the Shanxi Province. The inscribed character *Ningrui* means to gather auspice.

式。中国书法，是中国汉字特有的一种传统艺术，被誉为"无言的诗、无行的舞、无图的画、无声的乐"。

书法可谓无处不在，在中国画、中国扇、楹联、匾额、建筑、剪纸等实用物体或艺术作品上都能看到书法的身影。优美的汉字不仅仅是一种装饰，更是一种文化的象征，古人用文字的形式表达美好的愿望。

characters are not only ornamental but serve as a cultural symbol, by which the ancients could express their best wishes.

The chirography of Chinese characters can broadly divide into archaic and modern style according to variation in momentum and posture of writing. The archaic style mainly includes oracle-bone inscription, bronze inscription, *Zhouwen* (resembling small seal script in style, yet having overlapping structures), and Ancient Script of the Six States, whereas the modern style includes small seal script, clerical script, cursive script, regular script and running script. Seal script, clerical script, cursive script, regular script and running script altogether constitute the five chirographies of Chinese characters and all have its own distinctive characteristics. The seal script is of primitive simplicity, the clerical script appears forthright and sincere, the cursive script looks dashing and elegant, the regular script features neatness, while the running script moves quite smoothly. The beauty of Chinese calligraphy is mainly reflected in brushwork of dots and strokes, the character configuration and the overall layout.

匾额、楹联

匾额是指挂在门楣、屋檐等处的装饰，上面大多写有建筑物的名称、性质或者表达感情等内容的文字。楹联是指挂在柱子上的对联。楹联上的文字或庄重，或飘逸，多写在木板或者竹片上。匾额和楹联是中国古代建筑装饰的重要手段，二者常常一同出现。

Bian'e (Horizontal Plaque) and *Yinglian* (Couplets Hung on the Hall Columns)

Bian'e is an ornamental plaque hanging on the lintels, eaves, etc. and mostly inscribed with the name of the building, its property or words expressive of emotions. *Yinglian* are couplets hung on the hall columns. Mostly written in boards or bamboo tablets, the characters can be either solemn or elegant. *Bian'e* and *Yinglian* are both important means for Chinese ancient architectural decoration and often appear together.

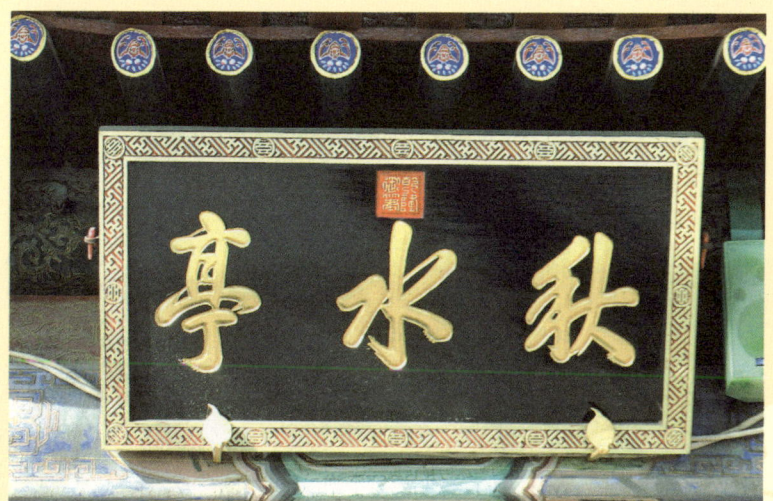

- 北京颐和园"秋水亭"匾额
  Bian'e Inscribed with "Autumn Water Pavilion" in the Summer Palace, Beijing

- "万寿无疆"匾额
  Bian'e Inscribed with "May You Have Longevity"

- 北京故宫中和殿悬挂着清代乾隆皇帝亲笔题写的匾额、楹联
  Bian'e and *Yinglian* Inscribed by Emperor Qianlong of the Qing Dynasty (1616-1911) Hanging in the Hall of Central Harmony at the Imperial Palace, Beijing

汉字的书体变化主要是指汉字笔势和体态的变化，分为古体和近体。古体包括甲骨文、金文、籀文、六国古文；近体包括小篆、隶书、草书、楷书、行书等。其中篆书、隶书、楷书、行书、草书构成了中国书法的五种字体，每种字体都有各自鲜明的特征，篆书古朴、隶书率真、草书潇洒、楷书工整、行书流畅。汉字的书法之美主要体现在点画用笔、结体取势以及章法布局三方面。

点画用笔之美

点画即文字的笔画，其外形有肥瘦、长短、方圆、曲直、断连等区别，其质地又有刚柔、强弱、浓淡等不同。用笔即用笔的方法，也

Beauty of Strokes and Dots in Brushwork

The strokes of Chinese characters may vary both in appearance and in texture. In appearance, some strokes look fat, some lean; some long, some short, some round, some square; some straight, some curved; some connected, some broken. Likewise in texture, some strokes appear rigid, some flexible; some strong, some weak; some deep in shade, some light. The way to wield the brush, known as brush usage among the ancients, is now commonly referred to as brushwork. Brushwork also contains variation in movement, like lift and press, progress and retrogress, turn and break, rise and fall, slow and rapid, etc.

By certain writing techniques, calligraphers can bring out a variety of

- "汉"字由隶书、楷体、行体到草体的演变
  Evolution of the Chinese Character "汉" (*Han* means an ethnic group or a dynasty of China, and has other meanings) from Clerical Script, Regular Script, Running Script to Cursive Script

叫"运笔",现在普遍称其为"笔法",包含提按、逆顺、转折、顿挫、迟速等变化。

点画用笔就是运用一定的技巧书写各种各样的笔画形态,形成不同的艺术效果。每种书体都有不一样的点画用笔方法,同一种书体的点画用笔根据书写者自身风格的不

strokes and thus result in diverse artistic effects. Different chirographies also differ in brushwork. Actually even one chirography may have variable strokes in accordance with personal style of the calligrapher. A good control of the strokes or a good knowledge of the brushwork to a great extent decides the fineness of a calligraphic

- 《白氏草堂记》邓石如(清)

  邓石如(1743—1805),清代著名书法家。此作品是其篆书代表作。小篆的笔画粗细均匀,文字书写顺畅,排列方正,给人一种整齐划一的美感。小篆这一字体在书法界具有一定的地位,受到广大书法家和书法爱好者的喜爱。

  Thatched Cottage of the Bai Family, by Deng Shiru (Qing Dynasty, 1616-1911)

  Deng Shiru (1743-1805) is a famous Chinese calligrapher during the Qing Dynasty. *Thatched Cottage of the Bai Family* is his masterpiece of seal script. The strokes are uniform in thickness. The characters, foursquare arranged, all move smoothly and give an aesthetic sense of neatness. The seal script holds an important position in the calligraphy world, having been pursued and adopted by a majority of calligraphers and calligraphy enthusiasts.

点画八病

点画八病,即在书法学习中,没有掌握基本的点画、运笔规律,因此出现各种病态的点画。元代书法家李溥光在其著作《雪庵永字八法》中说到点画八病,即"牛头、鼠尾、蜂腰、鹤膝、竹节、棱角、折木、柴担"。

牛头指作点时用力太大,或笔没有提按,导致锋角显露又臃肿。鼠尾指下笔时粗重而到笔画末端时,突然变细,轻飘而行。蜂腰指作背抛转折时,中间圆转处笔画变细,而抛出处又变粗,上下呈脱节状。鹤膝指转折处用笔过重或笔没有提起,使折处肥大突出。竹节指笔画中间细,而两头粗重,比例失调。棱角指起笔、转笔或收笔时棱角尖细显露。折木指没有起笔、收笔的笔画,粗野破碎。柴担指横画两头低下,中间隆起,分曲过分。

Eight Faults in Brushwork

In calligraphic studies, if one does not grasp the basic rules of brushwork, there will appear a variety of morbid strokes, in particular the common eight faults. Li Puguang (self-titled name, Xue'an) , a calligrapher of the Yuan Dynasty (1206-1368) once referred to the eight faults in his work *Xue'an's Eight Principles of Character Yong*. They are vividly named as "ox head, mouse tail, wasp waist, crane knee, bamboo joint, pointed angle, broken wood, and shoulder-pole for firewood."

Ox head means to dot too hard, or one does not lift the brush before pressing, hence leaving a sharp and swollen angle in the stroke. Mouse tail, as the name suggests, refers to a heavy and thick brushwork at the beginning which however, suddenly turns thin and light in the end. If the stroke looks like wasp waist, it is because at the rotating point the stroke is thin, but turns thicker when thrown out, thus out of line with the former part. The fault of crane knee also appears in the turning point which tumidly juts out due to heavy brushwork or no lifting of the wrist. Bamboo joint refers to imbalance between the thin middle part of the stroke and its two heavy ends. The fault of pointed or tapered angle usually appears at the beginning, turning point and end of the stroke. Broken wood refers to a stroke with neither beginning nor end, boorish and fragmented. The last fault usually happens to the horizontal stroke with two ends drooping downward and the middle part bulging up, just like a shoulder-pole for firewood.

同也有所差异。掌握了用笔，也就掌握了书法的点画线条，这是决定书法优秀的关键所在。好的书法，其点画用笔一定是生动、立体、富有美感的。如果没有掌握好点画用笔方法，出现"点画八病"，那么就一定写不出好的书法作品。

work. Excellent calligraphy usually features vivid, three-dimensional and pretty strokes. If one does not grasp the essentials of brushwork or gets involved with any of the eight faults listed blow, then you cannot produce a good calligraphic work.

- "之"字
  书写极具张力，笔画粗细对比强烈。
  The Chinese Character *Zhi* (Zigzag)
  The brushwork is full of tension. The strokes strongly contrast with each other in thickness.

- 《神策军碑》柳公权（唐）
  柳公权（778—865），唐代著名书法家，楷书四大家之一。此作品为楷体，用笔以方为主，兼施圆笔，出锋爽健，字体峻峭，"之"字颇为典型。
  ***Shence Imperial Guard Monument*, by Liu Gongquan (Tang Dynasty, 618-907)**
  Liu Gongquan (778-865), the famous calligrapher of the Tang Dynasty, is one of the Four Masters of Regular Script. This calligraphy work in regular script is mainly square and also round brushwork. The stroke looks clear and sturdy; the chirography appears vigorous and abrupt. The character *Zhi* (zigzag) is a typical example.

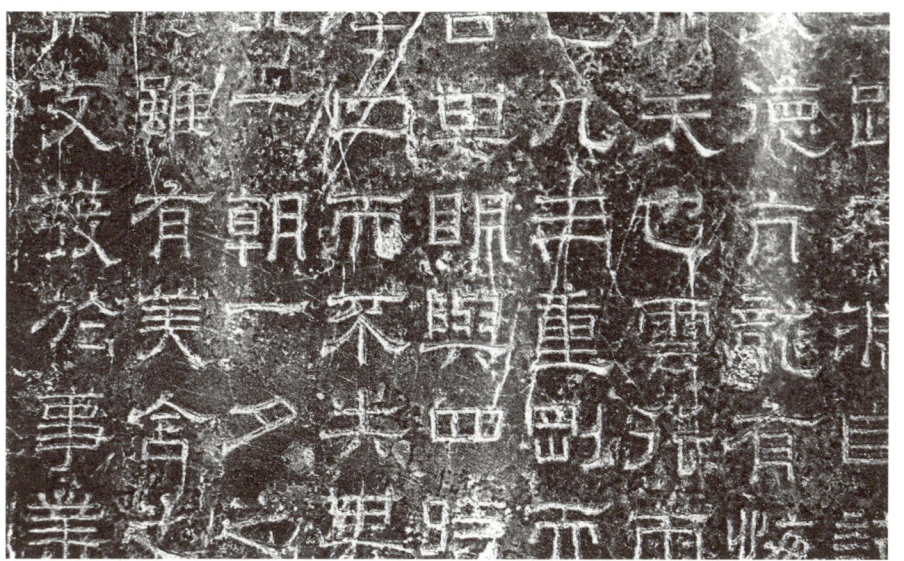

- 熹平石经（东汉）

东汉熹平年间（172—178）刻在石头上的隶书体儒学经典作品，世称"熹平石经"。隶书的运笔有"蚕头雁尾"之称。长画起笔时，回锋隆起，形如"蚕头"；横波收笔时，顿笔斜起，形如"雁尾"。

Xiping Stone Classics (Eastern Han Dynasty, 25-220)

Xiping Stone Classics is a collection of stone carved books on various Confucian classics in clerical script during Xiping Period (172-178) of the Eastern Han Dynasty. The clerical script is also noted as "silkworm head and wild goose tail" due to its distinctive shape. The calligrapher starts with a horizontal line, then retrogrades and lifts the brush, shaping the stroke like the silkworm head. Then the brush pauses and moves downward-diagonal, so the end looks like the flared tail of the wild goose.

楷书四大家
Four Masters of the Regular Script

　　唐朝的欧阳询、颜真卿、柳公权以及元朝的赵孟頫合称为"楷书四大家"，也称"四大楷书"。四者皆以楷书著称，但书体风格又各不相同，分别被称为欧体、颜体、柳体以及赵体。

　　Ouyang Xun, Yan Zhenqing, Liu Gongquan of the Tang Dynasty (618-907), and Zhao Mengfu of the Yuan Dynasty (1206-1368) are together known as "Four Masters of the Regular Script", or

"Four Regular Scripts" for short. All of them outshine in regular script yet differ from each other in style. Their chirographies are respectively referred to as Ou style, Yan style, Liu style and Zhao style.

欧阳询（557—641），唐代书法家、书法理论家。其楷书法度严谨，笔力险劲，被称为唐人楷书第一。其楷书代表作《九成宫醴泉铭》最为著名。欧阳询还著有《传授诀》《用笔论》《八诀》《三十六法》等，总结了书法用笔、结体、章法等书法的形式技巧和美学要求。

Ouyang Xun (557-641) is a calligrapher and calligraphy theorist of the Tang Dynasty. His regular script retains rigor and vigor, hence exalted as the foremost of all regular scripts in the Tang

● 欧阳询画像
Portrait of Ouyang Xun

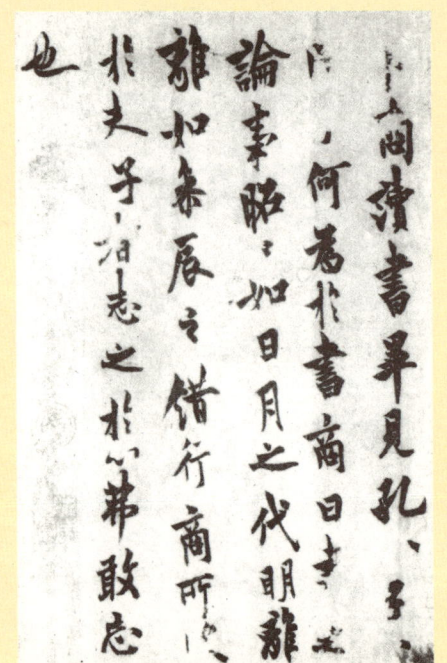

● 《卜商帖》欧阳询（唐）
Bu Shang's Copybook, by Ouyang Xun (Tang Dynasty, 618-907)

Dynasty. Among all his masterpieces in regular script, *Sweet Spring Inscription at Jiucheng Palace* is widely considered the best. Besides, his other works like *Teaching Art*, *Theory of Brushwork*, *Eight Knacks*, *Thirty-six Laws*, sum up the skills and aesthetic requirements of the brush movement, character configuration and composition of the writing.

颜真卿（708—784），唐代著名书法家。其书法筋力丰厚，字体丰腴，结体宽博而气势恢宏，骨力遒劲而气概凛然。他与柳公权并称"颜柳"，有"颜筋柳骨"之誉。

Yan Zhenqing (708-784) is another famous calligrapher of the Tang Dynasty. His writing appears energetic and well-rounded in form. The characters are

● 颜真卿画像
Portrait of Yan Zhenqing

● 《多宝塔碑》颜真卿（唐）
Duobao Pagoda Monument, by Yan Zhenqing (Tang Dynasty, 618-907)

all broadly configured, revealing a magnanimous and stern air. Yan Zhenqing and Liu Gongquan are together known as "Master Yan and Liu". People all sing highly of their calligraphy, comparing their regular script to bone and muscle.

柳公权（778—865），唐代著名书法家。其书法以骨力劲健见长，与颜真卿并称为"颜筋柳骨"。其书法体势劲媚，骨力道健，结体道劲，字字严谨。他的书法作品主要有《大唐回元观钟楼铭》《金刚经》《玄秘塔碑》《神策军碑》等。

Liu Gongquan (778-865) is also a famed calligrapher of the Tang Dynasty. His brushwork is marked with strength and power. Closely comparable to that of Yan Zhenqing, his handwriting oozes vigor and charm. The configuration of characters also appears firm and rigorous. His famous calligraphy works include *Inscription Carved on Bell-tower of the Huiyuan Temple in the Tang Dynasty*, *Diamond Sutra*, *Mysterious Pagoda Monument*, *Shence Imperial Guard Monument*, etc.

● 柳公权画像
Portrait of Liu Gongquan

● 《玄秘塔碑》柳公权（唐）
Mysterious Pagoda Monument, by Liu Gongquan (Tang Dynasty, 618-907)

赵孟頫（1254—1322），元代著名画家、书法家。其书法作品中的行楷（介于楷书与行书之间的字体）较多，大多用笔精到，结字严谨，《赤壁赋》堪称经典。

Zhao Mengfu (1254-1322) is a well-known painter and calligrapher of the Yuan Dynasty. His chirography mostly goes between the regular script and running script. His brushwork manifests precision and stern configuration. *Ode to the Red Cliff* is one of his masterpieces.

- 赵孟頫画像
  Portrait of Zhao Mengfu

- 《洛神赋》赵孟頫（元）
  Ode to the Goddess of the Luo River, by Zhao Mengfu (Yuan Dynasty, 1206-1368)

天下三大行书
Three Great Running Scripts in China

　　行书将书法艺术中的气韵神采、筋骨血肉表现得淋漓尽致，达到了刚柔、方圆、虚实等形式的对立统一。在中国书法历史中，诞生了许多杰出的行书作品，其中王羲之的《兰亭序》、颜真卿的《祭侄文稿》、苏轼的《黄州寒食帖》被誉为"天下三大行书"。

Running script brings the artistic effect and vitality of the calligraphy to full play, and presents the unity of opposites, like hard and soft, square and round, realistic and idealistic. In Chinese history countless masters gave birth to numerous outstanding calligraphic works, among which, Wang Xizhi's *Preface to the Orchid Pavilion*, Yan Zhenqing's *Manuscript in Memory of Nephew Yan Jiming*, and Su Shi's *Cold Food Observance in Huangzhou City* are collectively lauded as the "Three Great Running Scripts in China".

天下第一行书——晋·王羲之《兰亭序》

　　晋代著名书法家王羲之（321—379）被尊为"书圣"。《兰亭序》又名《兰亭集序》，是王羲之与文人墨客在绍兴兰亭饮酒赋诗时所作，记述了兰亭周围的山水之美和聚会的欢乐之情。此书法作品通篇笔势纵横，意气酣畅，如龙跳虎卧，浑然天成。轻重疾徐，疏密斜正，敛放揖让，承接呼应。传说此帖受到唐太宗李世民（599—649）的钟爱，真迹随其陪葬，遂失传人间。

• **王羲之画像**

王羲之（321—379），东晋（317—420）书法家，被称为"书圣"。《兰亭集序》有"天下第一行书"的美称。

Portrait of Wang Xizhi

Wang Xizhi (321-379) is a famous calligrapher of the Eastern Jin Dynasty (317-420) traditionally respected as "the Sage of Calligraphy". *Preface to the Orchid Pavilion* has been honored as "the First Great Running Script in China".

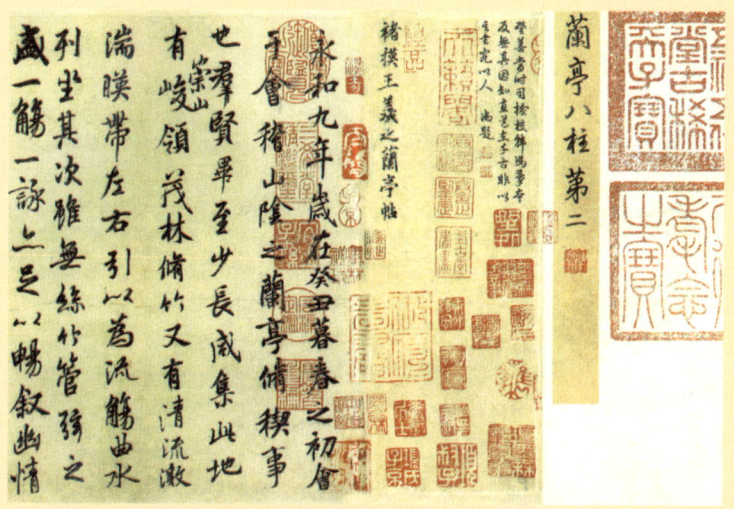

- 王羲之《兰亭序》（褚遂良摹）
  Wang Xizhi's *Preface to the Orchid Pavilion* Copied by Chu Suiliang

The First Great Running Script in China—*Preface to the Orchid Pavilion*, by Wang Xizhi of the Eastern Jin Dynasty

Wang Xizhi (321-379) is a famous calligrapher of the Eastern Jin Dynasty traditionally respected as "the Sage of Calligraphy". *Preface to the Orchid Pavilion* was written when he and other men of letters composed poems over wine near the Orchid Pavilion of Shaoxing City. It describes a joyful gathering immersed in the beauty of surrounding landscapes. This calligraphic work features unrestrained handwriting, and free spirit. With unbridled vigor, this work of nature is of highest quality and especially well-balanced in brush movement, neither heavy nor light, neither fast nor slow, neither sparse nor dense. The slanting and upright strokes run smoothly, echo and make way for each other. This piece of work is said to be particularly beloved by Li Shimin (599-649), Emperor Taizong of the Tang Dynasty and even buried with him. Now the authentic work has been lost. Running script in this copybook flows quite smoothly. Both the strokes and the graphic posture are set out most vividly.

天下第二行书——唐·颜真卿《祭侄文稿》

唐代著名书法家颜真卿（708—784），《祭侄文稿》是其为祭奠自己的侄子颜季明所作。这篇书法作品体现出颜真卿书写时的感情起伏，起首凝重，篇末忘情。

- 《兰亭序》正文中的"之"字

  全文共21个"之"字，其中正文中有20个，变化多姿，无一雷同，真正达到一种随心所欲而不逾矩的境界。

  The Chinese Character *Zhi* (Zigzag) in the *Preface to the Orchid Pavilion*

  Zhi appears altogether 21 times in the *Preface to the Orchid Pavilion* and 20 times in the body of the text, but all vary from each other. The writer willfully followed his own inclination yet never went beyond the boundary.

开篇书写时，字体大小匀称，浓纤得体。随着言词的深入，行书、草书渐趋相杂，字形时大时小，行距忽宽忽窄，笔锋有藏有露。

The Second Great Running Script in China—*Manuscript in Memory of Nephew Yan Jiming*, by Yan Zhenqing of the Tang Dynasty

Yan Zhenqing (708-784) is a well-known calligrapher of the Tang Dynasty. *Manuscript in Memory of Nephew Yan Jiming*, just as the title indicates, is a memorial work that betrays the deep emotion of the writer from the dignified beginning to the cool end of the text. The calligrapher starts with characters of even size and well-proportioned thickness. As the emotion goes deeper, running script and cursive script begin to mix with each other. The font size and line spacing vary from time to time. The tip of the brush likewise is now hidden, now exposed.

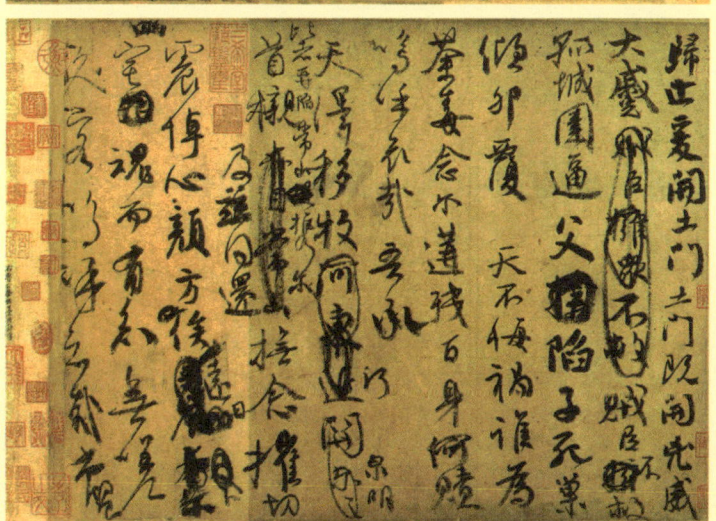

- **《祭侄文稿》**
  用笔果敢，毫无迟滞之迹，又不乏沉着，是独树一帜的颜真卿式笔法。
  Manuscript in Memory of Nephew Yan Jiming
  The brushwork turns out bold without any trace of hesitation or any lack of composure. This technique of writing is unique to Yan Zhenqing himself.

天下第三行书——北宋·苏轼《黄州寒食帖》

北宋著名文学家、书法家苏轼（1037—1101），号东坡居士，又称"苏东坡"。因作诗讥刺朝廷而被贬谪。这篇《黄州寒食帖》是他在宋神宗元丰二年（1079）被贬为黄州团练副使时所书行草。寒食即寒食节，清明节的前一天。这一天各家禁烟火，只吃冷食。通篇起伏跌宕，恣肆飞扬，痛快淋漓，一气呵成。

The Third Great Running Script in China—*Cold Food Observance in Huangzhou City*, by Su Shi of the Northern Song Dynasty

Su Shi (1037-1101) is a famous scholar and calligrapher of the Northern Song Dynasty. His pseudonym was *Dongpo Jushi*, so people often refer to him as Su Dongpo. As his poem involves derision of the government, he was banished from the imperial court. *Cold Food Observance in Huangzhou City* is a calligraphic work in semi-cursive script written in the Yuanfeng Period, i.e. the second year (1079) during the reign of Emperor Shenzong of the Northern Song Dynasty. Then he was exiled to Huangzhou and served as the deputy commander of local troops. The Cold Food Festival falls one day before the Pure Brightness (*Qingming*) Festival. On that day, the setting of fire is forbidden in every household and all food is to be consumed cold. This work is characterized by flowing rhythm, unrestrained brushwork and dripping passion, as if accomplished in one go.

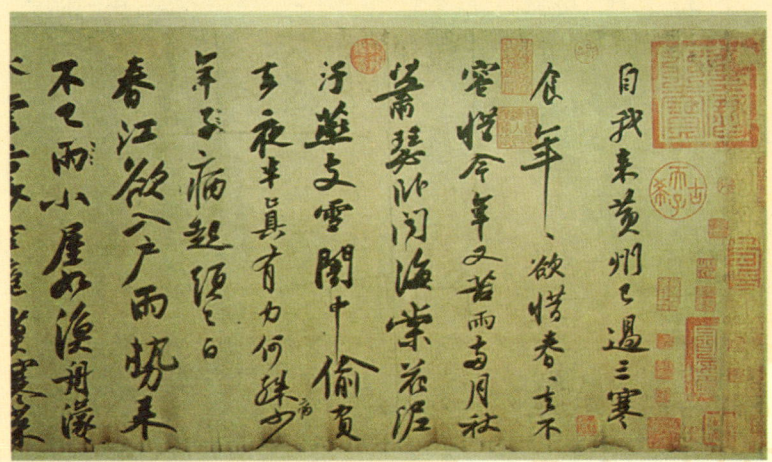

- 《黄州寒食帖》
  此帖点画之中，正锋侧锋转换多变，顺手断连，浑然天成。

  Cold Food Observance in Huangzhou City
  In this copybook, the writer now centers the brush tip and slants it, breaks the stroke and connects it, making the calligraphy a work of nature.

结体取势之美

结体取势是指书法写作者通过一定的结体技巧，根据各自的审美情趣来塑造汉字的理想体势。结体，又称"结字"，指汉字书写的间架结构。通过对汉字点画进行疏密、聚散、正斜、高低等处理，使得字体的骨架更富有美感。文字的骨架，就好比支撑着建筑的立柱，是立字的根本所在。体势，指文字

Beauty of Character Configuration

Jieti Qushi (literally meaning to decide the form based on the structure) refers to the ideal posture of a character accomplished by certain configuration technique and calligrapher's aesthetic taste. To be specific, character configuration mainly deals with the organic combination of strokes and dots, including their density and height, meeting and parting, upright and slanting,

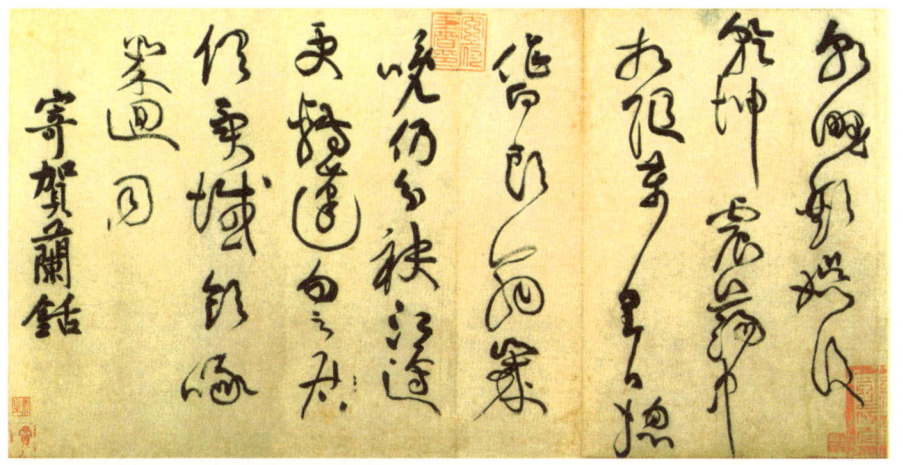

- 《书杜甫寄贺兰铦诗》黄庭坚（北宋）

  黄庭坚（1045—1105），北宋诗人、词人、书法家。此帖为黄庭坚的狂草代表作，结体移形变位，字迹俯仰敧侧，字势动静相宜。

  Copybook of Du Fu's Song for Helan Xian, by Huang Tingjian (Northern Song Dynasty, 960-1127)

  Huang Tingjian (1045-1105) is a poet and calligrapher of the Northern Song Dynasty. This calligraphic work is his masterpiece of wild cursive script. The configuration is full of change, the characters tilt now forward, now backward, and the movement of brushwork also strikes the equipoise between static and dynamic.

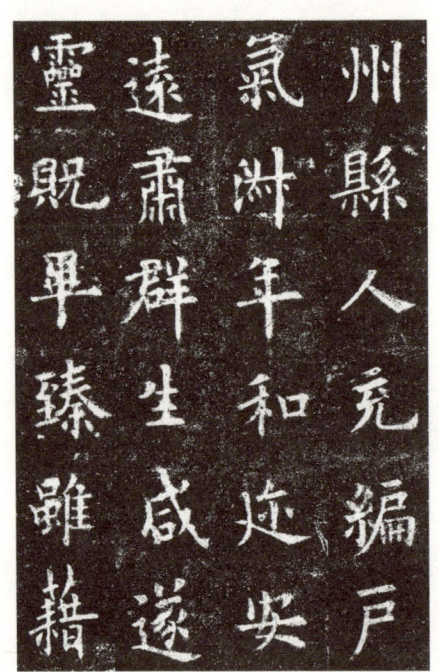

- **《九成宫醴泉铭》[局部] 欧阳询（唐）**

此碑刻作品被后世喻为"天下第一楷书"。其结体以纵势为主，在整体的肃穆之中，局部的险势起到了点睛作用，避免了单纯的严肃而导致的呆板。

Part of *Sweet Spring Inscription at Jiucheng Palace*, by Ouyang Xun (Tang Dynasty, 618-907)

This stone tablet is later hailed as "the Best Regular Script in China". The character configuration mostly inclines downward and gives a stern impression. Yet the partial high-abrupt arrangement provides the finishing touch that helps avoid the possible dullness caused by sheer solemnity.

- **《三坟记》 李阳冰（唐）**

李阳冰，唐代著名书法家，《三坟记》是其小篆代表作品。此作品结体均匀、对称、平行，每个字大小一致，排列方正，横竖成行，十分顺畅和谐。篆书的笔画中没有"点"，横、竖及曲线等笔画构成了篆书。篆书字体上紧下松，体态修长，横平竖直，布白（指文字的间架、字与字之间以及行与行之间的布置）均匀，其中有许多字左右完全对称。

***Stele of Three Graves*, by Li Yangbing (Tang Dynasty, 618-907)**

Li Yangbing is a famous calligrapher of the Tang Dynasty. *Stele of Three Graves* is his representative work of small seal script. The handwriting is even, symmetric and parallel in structure. The characters are of uniform size, squarely arranged and distributed in harmony. In seal scripts, there are no dots, only horizontal, vertical and curving strokes. The chirography is slender in figure, tight in the upper part and loose in the lower. The straight horizontal and vertical strokes further contribute to the uniform structure. Indeed, the right and left parts of many characters are completely symmetrical.

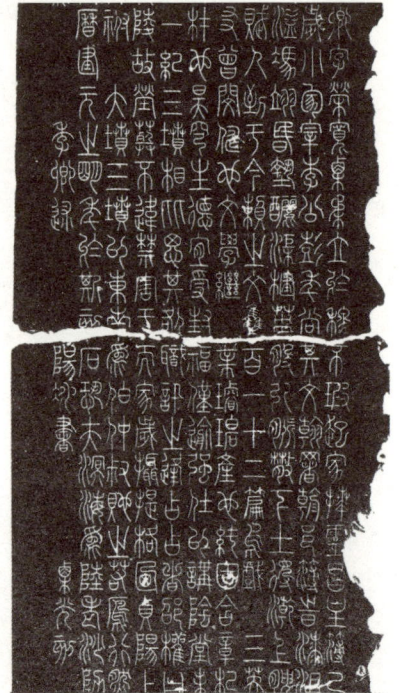

- 《隶书五言联》伊秉绶（清）

  伊秉绶（1754—1815），清代著名书法家，精于隶书。此作品字形扁阔，波磔飞动；长短字形疏密结合，呈现出张扬飘逸的动态美。

  Five-character Couplet in Clerical Script, by Yi Bingshou (Qing Dynasty, 1616-1911)

  Yi Bingshou (1754-1815) is a distinguished calligrapher of the Qing Dynasty. He is particularly skilled in the clerical script. In this couplets, the characters appear flat and broad in shape. The left-falling and right-falling strokes look like flying in posture. Characters of different height or length are well-blended in terms of density, hence radiating a dynamic grace.

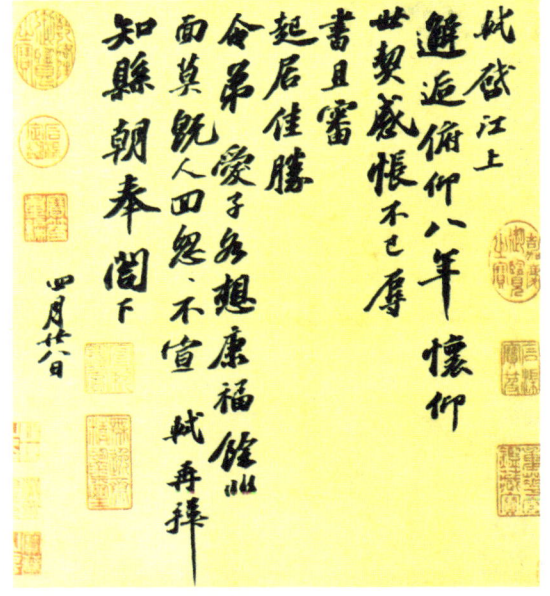

- 《江上帖》苏轼（北宋）

  苏轼与北宋书法家黄庭坚（1045—1105）、书画家米芾（1051—1107）、书法家蔡襄（1012—1067）齐名，合称"宋四家"。这篇行书作品富有丰秀雅逸的气息，结体以短肥为主要特点。

  Copybook of the River, by Su Shi (Northern Song Dynasty, 960-1127)

  Su Shi is another expert at calligraphy. Together with the great calligrapher Huang Tingjian (1045-1105), calligrapher and painter Mi Fu (1051-1107), calligrapher Cai Xiang (1012-1067), they are collectively known as the "Four Great Calligraphy Masters of the Song Dynasty". This work in running script is full of elegance. The characters are mostly short and fat in configuration.

的形体结构、气势风格。结体取势要做到层次分明、错落有致、形神并茂。

章法布局之美

章法布局与点画用笔、结体取势并称为书法技艺的三要素。章法布局，就是指书法作品通篇的整体经营，包括宏观、微观、形式、意

hence to render the frame of the character more attractive. The frame of a character, just like the beam of a house, is the foundation of writing. Posture refers to the structure, momentum and style of the character. In character configuration, the strokes should be well-arranged in picturesque order, at once embodying form and spirit.

Beauty of the Overall Layout

Strokes and dots in brushwork, character configuration and overall layout are together known as the three basic elements of calligraphic skills. The overall layout of a calligraphy work refers to its general design, both in macro and

- 《篆书临石鼓文轴》 吴昌硕（清）

吴昌硕（1844—1927），晚清书法家。此帖动静结合、正敧相生，字间距很小，字虽各不相连，却给人一种茂密严实、一气呵成的感觉，整体感十分强烈。每行字之间采用了绵密布局手法，活泼跳宕，笔致轻重完全根据正文篆书的疏密来布置。

Seal Script Imitation of Stone Drum Script, by Wu Changshuo (Qing Dynasty, 1616-1911)

Wu Changshuo (1844-1927) is a calligrapher of the late Qing Dynasty. This calligraphy work exemplifies a perfect combination of the static with the dynamic, the upright with the slanting. The characters are narrow in spacing but unconnected, giving a strong sense of density, coherence and wholeness, as if accomplished in one go. By the tight-knit technique, characters moves lively and freely in the line. The heaviness of the brushwork completely depends on the density of the seal script in the body of the text.

- 《隶书七言联》何绍基（清）

何绍基（1799—1873），清代诗人、画家、书法家，工于行书、草书、隶书、篆书。此作品通篇体势严整，笔法稳健，秀逸而又雄浑古朴。

Seven-character Couplet in Clerical Script, by He Shaoji (Qing Dynasty, 1616-1911)

He Shaoji (1799-1873) is a poet, painter and famous calligrapher of the Qing Dynasty. He is at once good at running script, cursive script, clerical script and seal script. This calligraphic work features neat posture and robust brushwork, oozing an elegant charm and simultaneously betraying a primitive simplicity.

境等方面，既有字符体势的塑造，又有字群的排布、行款的处理以及印章的施用。

　　首先，字与纸张的关系应该是黑白相应，大小相宜，疏密相称，宽窄适度，行间要透气，不能安排得太满，四周要留白。其次，首尾

micro levels, and from form to artistic conception. It includes posture shaping of individual characters, arrangement of the character group, pattern of the lines and application of the seal.

　　Firstly, the character and paper should be black and white, echoing in color. Characters should be appropriate in size, density and width, well distributed in the lines, neither too crowded nor too sparse, with some blank space left in the edges of the paper. Secondly, the first character should coordinate with the last in artistic effect. Generally, in regular script characters should be evenly written, whereas in running script and cursive script they should appear thick and sturdy. In addition, the characters should be of orderly arrangement whether they are horizontally or vertically arrayed. Regular script usually demands

遥相呼应，一般来说楷书通篇匀称，行书、草书则应粗壮厚重。再次，要做到行列有序，行气贯通。楷书要求行列相等，篆书要行宽列窄，隶书要行窄列宽。这三种书体都讲究横有行、竖有列，行列中的字，其中心要相互对应，处在同一条直线上。行书、草书虽然表面上看没有行列，但是安排有度，行气贯通，浑然天成，而非杂乱无章。

章法布局的好坏是衡量书法作品艺术价值高低的重要标准，也是

lines and rows of equal width; seal script requires wide lines and narrow rows, while the clerical script is quite the reverse. In short, all three chirographies are particular about lines and rows, insisting the center of characters should correspond with each other and stand in one straight line. As to the running script and cursive script, they seemingly have no lines or rows, but in fact coherently arranged and far from chaotic.

In brief, the overall layout is not only the important criterion to measure the artist value of a calligraphy work, but also the standard to measure the artistic

- 《古诗四帖》张旭（唐）

张旭（约685—759），唐代著名书法家，世称"草圣"，其草书与李白的诗歌、裴旻的剑舞并称"三绝"。此帖在布局上通篇大收大放，行文纵横跌宕，满纸如云烟缭绕。

Four Ancient Poems, by Zhang Xu (Tang Dynasty, 618-907)

Zhang Xu (ca.685-759) is a famous calligrapher of the Tang Dynasty hailed as "the Sage of Cursive Script". His cursive script, together with Li Bai's poems and Pei Min's swordsmanship, is collectively regarded as "the Three Highest Forms of Art" at that time. In layout, this calligraphic work moves freely in length and breadth. Characters fill the paper in flowing rhythm like mist wreathes the hilltop.

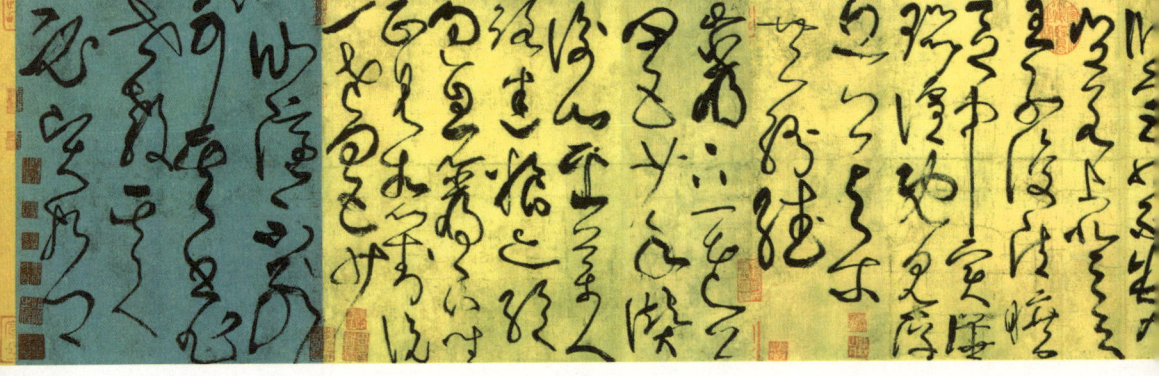

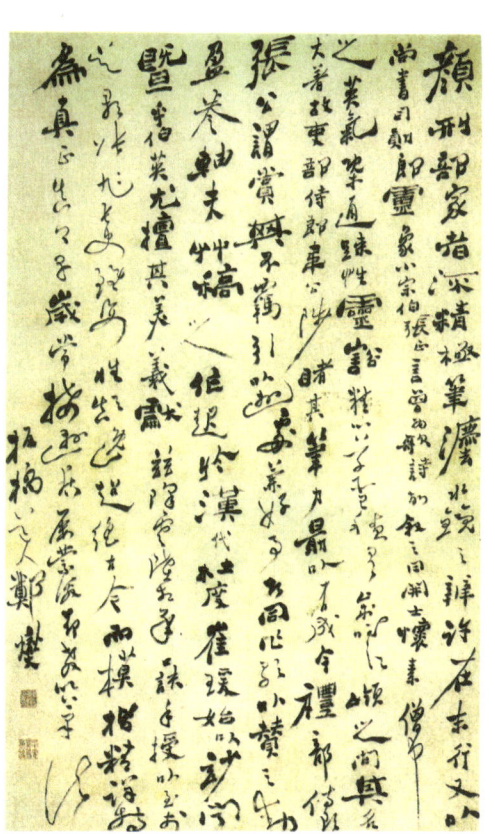

- 《行草论书诗轴》 郑燮（清）

  郑燮（1693—1765），号板桥，又称"郑板桥"，清代书法家、画家、文学家，独创"板桥体"。此轴虽然杂糅了很多形体，但布局丝毫未觉散乱，以乱石铺街之势将字撑满纸面，字与字之间腾挪揖让，行与行之间顾盼呼应，整体风格活泼古朴。

  Scroll on Poetry Writing in Semi-cursive Script, by Zheng Xie (Qing Dynasty, 1616-1911)

  Zheng Xie (1693-1765), whose pseudonym is Banqiao, hence also known as "Zheng Banqiao", is a great calligrapher, painter and scholar of the Qing Dynasty who invents "the Banqiao style". This scroll, though mingled with many things, does not look chaotic in layout. The characters crowd onto the paper like rocks scattering about the street. Nevertheless, characters all make way for each other, lines also echo in between, rendering the whole scroll lively and quaint.

081

优美的汉字 The Graceful Chinese Character

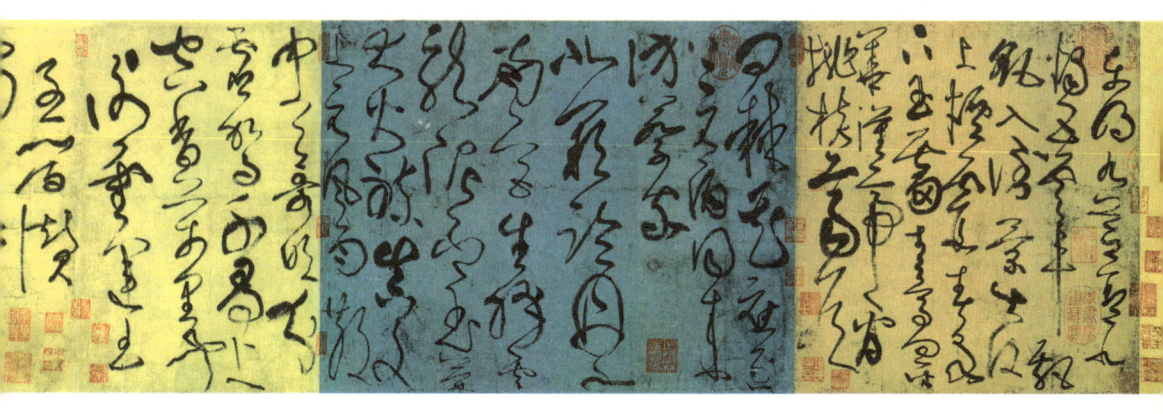

衡量书法家书法造诣深浅的重要标准。章法布局中的一个笔画、一个间距出现错误，就有可能影响整篇作品。

汉字的书法美在气势与意态，是一种抽象艺术之美。

attainments of a calligrapher. Even if the stroke or character spacing is slightly defected, the whole work would be impaired in quality.

The beauty of calligraphy primarily lies in the momentum and posture of the characters. It is an abstract art.

- 《老子道德经》鲜于枢（元）

鲜于枢（1246—1302），元代著名书法家。此作品整体风格清爽劲利，字体间距均匀，行气贯通，首尾一气。

Laozi's Tao Te Ching (*The Classic of the Virtue of the Tao*), by Xianyu Shu (Yuan Dynasty, 1206-1368)

Xianyu Shu (1256-1301) is a famous calligrapher of the Yuan Dynasty. This calligraphic work turns out refreshing and vigorous as a whole. The characters and lines are evenly spaced as if at one stroke, hence giving a coherent impression.

书法的学习

学习中国书法，需要掌握一些基本技巧。首先要注意的是拿笔的方法。书法的书写工具一般为毛笔，"五字执笔法"是执笔的方法之一，此法便于控制毛笔，用力均衡。五字执笔法分别指擫、押、钩、格、抵五种指法。擫，是大拇指按笔的指法，即用大拇指的指肚紧贴笔管内侧，与食指相对用力；押，是食指押笔的指法，即用食指的第一指节贴住笔管外侧，与拇指相对用力；钩，是中指钩笔的指法，即用中指弯曲的第一、第二指节弯曲勾住笔管的外侧；格，是无名指挡笔的指法，即用无名指的指甲处紧贴笔管，将向内钩回的笔管挡住；抵，是小指的托笔指法，即用小指托住上面的手指，以增加力量。

其次，需要注重运笔，这是书法最重要的基本功。运笔讲究笔画的提按、节奏、布局。书法讲究运笔，运笔要"活"，需临摹百家帖，各取所长。同时还要自然，不矫揉造作。即使结构再复杂的汉字，也是由基本的笔画组成的，学习书法就要扎扎实实地练好基本笔画。对于初学者来说，临摹名家书法范本的字帖是很好的方法。

再次，学习书法要注意写字的姿势。如果姿势不对，不光写不好字，对人的身体也不好。无论是坐着练字还是站着练字，头都要正，身体保持端正、挺直、放松。手腕、手臂的姿势尤其重要，常见的有三种：枕腕，即将左手平枕于右手腕下；提腕，即将右手提起，以肘部着案，或将左手垫于肘下；悬腕，即将手腕、手肘都悬空，靠手臂上部带动下部运笔。

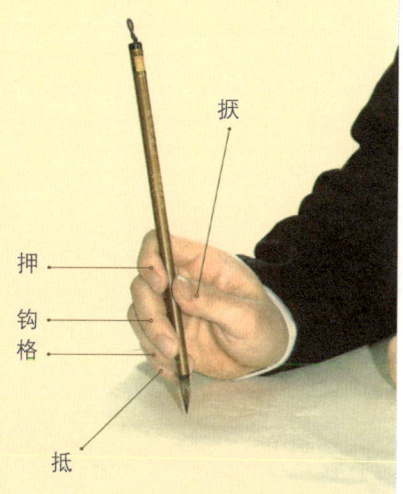

- 五字执笔法
  Five-character Method of Brush Holding

Calligraphy Learning

To learn Chinese calligraphy, one needs to grasp some basic skills. Firstly, you should know the right way to hold the tool, i.e., the writing brush. "Five-character Method of Brush Holding" is one of the many ways, which unlike the others, not only renders brush control much easier, but produces even strength in writing. This method includes five finger positions, respectively *Ye*, *Ya*, *Gou*, *Ge*, *Di*. *Ye* refers to the finger position of the thumb, i.e. using the thumb to hold the inner side of the brush and then putting forth strength together with the index finger. *Ya* refers to the position of the index finger. It keeps the first joint of the index finger close to the outer side of the shaft and then exerts strength together with the thumb. *Gou* refers to the use of the middle finger which bends twice to hook the outer side of the writing brush. *Ge* refers to the work of the ring finger, that is, to keep the fingernail close to the shaft and then push against the brush that is hooked inward. *Di* refers to the position of the little finger which supports and adds strength to the four fingers above.

Secondly, enough attention should be paid to the wielding of the writing brush, which is another basic skill in calligraphy learning. The brush wielding involves lifting and pressing of the strokes, rhythm of movement, and layout of the characters. It requires good flexibility as well as frequent imitation of excellent copybooks to absorb their individual merits. At the same time, the brushwork should appear natural rather than artificial. Even the most complicated character is made up of basic strokes, so in calligraphy learning one should first perfect the strokes as far as possible. For beginners, to imitate copybooks of famous calligraphers is a good starting point.

Thirdly, calligraphy learning also requires right writing posture. If the posture is incorrect, the writing not only looks unsightly but also does harm to one's health. When we practice calligraphy, whether sitting or standing, the head should be upright and the body remains comfortably straight. The posture of wrist and arm is above all important. We can use supported wrist method, cushioning the left hand below the wrist of the right hand; or raised wrist method, i.e. lifting the right hand and putting the elbow on the desk, or cushioning the left hand below the right elbow; or suspended wrist method, to suspend the wrist and elbow, and then wield the forearm to lead the brush movement.

- **米字格**

  米字格是中国书法临帖写仿的一种界格，方便初学者对照字帖的笔画、部位来练字。

  Grid

  Grid is a confined framework used in imitation of Chinese calligraphy. It facilitates the beginners' practice of strokes and radicals according to the copybook.

> 汉字与篆刻

中国篆刻是以篆书为主的书法与镌刻相结合制作印章的艺术，是汉字特有的艺术形式。2009年，中国篆刻同中国书法等项目一同入选联合国教科文组织《人类非物质文化遗产代表作名录》。篆刻与书法密切相关，因印面文字以篆书为主，故称"篆刻"。篆刻艺术，就是按照已经写好的书法或画好的图像，在金属、竹木、玉、石等印材上进行镌刻，具有欣赏和实用价值的艺术。因其以制作印章为主，又称"印章艺术"。篆刻经历了漫长的发展过程，万千气象纳于方寸之间，向来为历代文人墨客所钟爱。人们或自篆自用，或馈赠文友，钤记落款，观赏把玩，以获得深厚的审美愉悦和艺术享受。

> Chinese Characters and Seal Carving

Chinese seal carving is a unique art form born out of the combination of calligraphy (mainly seal script) and carving. Chinese seal carving and Chinese calligraphy are closely related. In 2009, these two forms of art were selected by the UNESCO onto the *Representative Work List of Human Intangible Cultural Heritage*. As characters are mainly carved in seal script, the art is named seal carving. Detailedly speaking, craftsmen carve the written calligraphy or painted images onto receptive substances like metal, bamboo, wood, jade, stone, etc. and thus result in a work of art with both artistic and practical value. As the process mainly centers upon seal carving, seal carving is also known as seal art. After a long course of development, this art can arrange abundant images onto

- **各式各样的精美印章**
  印章作为艺术品，其价值一般表现在两个方面，一是其外形设计，二是印面文字的书法和镌刻艺术。

  Various Kinds of Exquisite Seals
  As a work of art, the value of seals is generally manifested in two aspects, its exterior design, and the quality of calligraphy and engraving on the surface of the seal.

篆刻由来已久，笔意劲秀的殷商甲骨文就是用刀刻在龟甲兽骨上的。古时，篆写作"瑑"，因凡是刻在玉石上的花纹都叫做"瑑"。后来，竹帛成为主要的书写工具，因而"瑑"改写为"篆"。在古代，凡是玉、石、竹、铜等材料上的雕刻都可以称为"篆刻"。汉代

one little device, therefore is beloved by literati of all ages. They either carved seals for their own use, or as gift for friends inscribed with one's signature, or simply for appreciation, to enjoy its great aesthetic beauty.

Seal carving appeared as early as in the Shang Dynasty (1600 B.C-1046 B.C) when the vigorous and awesome oracle-

印章

　　印章，指用作印于文件上表示鉴定或签署的工具，也指印章印出来的痕迹。篆刻印章在中国有着悠久的历史，篆刻艺术史可以上溯到2000多年前的春秋战国时代，这一阶段，篆刻的印章称为"玺"，古玺分官、私两类，当时不分尊卑都称为"玺"。玺文分边栏宽阔的朱文和有界格的白文两种，其内容包括官职、姓名、吉语和肖形图案等。古玺的形状、大小不一，有长方形、方形、圆形和其他各种异形。因被视为权力和凭证的信物，其材质也有所不同。

　　秦始皇统一中国之后，规定"玺"乃天子专用，其他人的印章统称为"印"。

- **不同形状的古代印章**
  古人讲究佩印，因此玺印大多有纽，在纽上穿孔系绶挂于腰间。印纽有各种不同形状，例如龙形、龟形、牛形、鹿形等等。

  Ancient Seals in Different Shapes
  The ancients liked wearing seals, so most *Xi* has buttons, by which the seal can be tied to the waist. The buttons also vary in shape. Some look like loong, some turtle; some are cow-shaped, some deer-shaped, etc.

● 丁仁印章（清）
Ding Ren's Seal (Qing Dynasty, 1616-1911)

● 乾隆皇帝青玉"八征耄念之宝"玺（清）
Gray Jade Treasure *Xi* for Celebration of Emperor Qianlong's Eightieth Birthday (Qing Dynasty, 1616-1911)

汉代是玺印空前发展的时期，官印称"章"或"印章"，私印称"信印"或"印信"。从古代印章发展而来的明清篆刻，距今也已经有近500年的历史。古代印章以独特的风貌和高度的艺术性，为篆刻艺术奠定了优良的基础。

Seal

Seal is a general name for printing stamps or impressions that are used in lieu of signatures or to prove authenticity of documents. The art of seal carving has a long history in China, which can date back to the Spring and Autumn Period and Warring States Period almost 2000 years ago. In the ancient times, regardless of hierarchy the engraved seal is all called *Xi* no matter it is for official use or private use. Characters carved on the seal can be in relief with wide space in the edge, or in intaglio limited in grids, with contents ranging from official posts, names, to auspicious words and sketchy graphics. Various in size, the ancient seals are carved into different shapes like rectangular, square, round, etc. They are also made of different materials, serving as a symbol of power and keepsake.

After Qin Shihuang (the First Emperor of the Qin Dynasty) unified China, he ordained that only the royal seals were called *Xi*, and others *Yin*. The Han Dynasty (206 B.C.-220 A.D.) witnessed the prosperous development of seal carving. At that time, the official seals were often referred to as *Zhang* or *Yinzhang* and the private ones *Xinyin* or *Yinxin*. Evolved from the ancient seals, modern seal carving appeared in the Ming Dynasty and Qing Dynasty (1368-1911) and has a history of nearly 500 years. In brief, the ancient seals, with its unique style and high degree of artistry, lay a solid foundation for the seal carving art.

• 白玉"大清受命之宝"玺（清）
White Jade "Imperial Treasure of Order-receive" *Xi* (Qing Dynasty, 1616-1911)

王莽（前45—23）定六书时，将印面上的文字称为"缪篆"，从此确定篆书为印章、印文的使用字体。唐宋之际，仍以篆书作印。明清两代，篆刻便成为以篆书为基础、利用雕刻方法在印面中表现疏密离合的艺术形态。篆刻从广义的雕镂铭刻变为治印之学。

篆刻的书体一般以大篆、小篆和汉篆为主，此外，还有隶书、楷书、行书等。明清之际，许多印章

- 摹印篆印文"商库"（秦）

  摹印篆是秦代印章篆书的一种，与小篆有所区别，其笔画平直，形体略方。

  Impression of *Shangku* (Commercial Storehouse) in *Mo* Seal Script (Qin Dynasty, 221 B.C.-206 B.C.)

  Mo seal script is one type of the seal script in the Qin Dynasty. Different from the small seal script, it has straight strokes and slightly square forms.

bone inscriptions were carved on tortoise shells and animal bones. At that time, the character for seal "篆" (*Zhuan*) is written otherwise "瑑" (*Zhuan*). This character has *Yu* (jade) as its radical, hence referring to all patterns carved on jade stones. Later, as silk and bamboo became the major writing materials, people began to use the character "篆" (having the radical of *Zhu* meaning bamboo) instead of "瑑". In any case, for the ancients all carvings on jade, stone, bamboo or bronze can be called "seal carving". In the Western Han Dynasty when Wang Mang (45 A.D.-23 B.C.) defined the Six Categories of Chinese Characters, characters on the seal were known as "*Mou* seal script". From then on, seal script was particularly used in seal printing till the Tang and Song dynasties (618-1279). During the Ming and Qing dynasties (1368-1911), seal carving began to combine the seal script with the carving technique, hence to achieve the artistic effect of graceful spacing on the seal surface. As well, seal carving no longer refers to engraving in broad sense but becomes a particular study of seal making.

The scripts commonly used in seal carving mainly includes large seal script, small seal script, and Han seal

- 鸟虫书印文"日利"（汉）

  鸟虫书是将篆书的笔画处理成鸟虫等动物的形态，因此得名，是古代一种美术化的文字。

  Impression of *Rili* (Good Day) in Bird-and-Insect Script (Han Dynasty, 206 B.C.-220 A.D.)

  Bird-and-insect script is thus named because it refines the strokes of seal script into the shape of animals like birds and insects. It is an ancient manner to beautify characters.

- 缪篆印文"皇后之玺"（汉）

  缪篆的字体不同于以往的秦篆，是笔画经过处理的文字，是汉印当中的主流字体。

  Impression of *Xi of the Empress* in *Mou* Seal Script (Han Dynasty, 206 B.C.-220 A.D.)

  Mou seal script diverges from the previous seal script of the Qin Dynasty. Its strokes are further manipulated. In the Han Dynasty, most seals were engraved with this kind of script.

- 九叠文印文"亲军侍卫将军随征四营关防"（明）

  九叠文又称"九叠篆"，最早见于唐代官印，其文字造型的突出特点为笔画反复折叠，充满整个印面，达到匀称整齐的效果。

  Impression of *General of Royal Army Which Guard the Four Frontier Military Camps* in Multi-folded Script (Ming Dynasty, 1368-1644)

  Multi-folded script, also known as multi-folded seal characters, first appeared on the official seal of the Tang Dynasty (618-907). In form, the strokes of the character are repeatedly folded to fill the entire seal surface, hence achieving a symmetric effect.

大家以自己创造的独具风貌的篆书入印，形成了众多流派。中国的篆刻艺术之所以丰富多彩，一个重要的因素就是印文的形体美，主要表现在线条和章法两方面。

线条之美

篆刻与书法有异曲同工之妙，也有笔法、章法等方面的讲究，只不过两者使用的工具不同，前者为毛笔，后者为刀。在印章上镌刻不同于在纸上书写，其难度更高。篆刻印章，首先需要懂得汉字的相

- **春秋战国时期的玺印**
  春秋战国时期的玺印，印文线条奇诡多姿。
  Xi (Seal) of the Spring and Autumn Period and Warring States Period (770 B.C.-221 B.C.)
  The impression of seals in the Spring and Autumn Period and Warring States Period usually reveals strange and varied lines.

script (of the style of the Han Dynasty), but clerical script, regular script and running script are also adopted from time to time. During the Ming and Qing dynasties (1368-1911), many great seal carvers invented their own unique style of seal script, hence forming numerous schools of seal carving. As to why the art of seal carving flourishes in China, one important factor is the physical beauty of the seal impression, especially with regard to the lines and layout.

Beauty of Lines

Similar to calligraphy, seal carving is also particular about the writing technique and composition. They simply employ different tools: the former uses brush, the latter knife. Besides, it is more difficult to carve on seals than write on paper. First, seal carving requires a good knowledge of Chinese characters (especially seal script), including the origin, evolution and structure of different chirographies, as well as the writing method of seal script, so that one can arrange the characters properly onto the seal surface. Second, some calligraphic skills are also necessary for good control of the lines of the character. In seal carving, the knife works just like the brush in calligraphy.

关知识，尤其是篆书，要了解字体的源流、结构，掌握篆书的书写方法，才能够将文字正确地组合在印面上。其次，还要有一定的书法基础，要求掌握文字的线条。篆刻讲求以书法入刻，刀中见笔，笔中见刀。印面上的文字线条既要曲直适宜、纵横得法，又要笔画精到、结体自如，呈现出一定的审美情趣。

The lines of the character should be neither straight nor curved too much. The horizontal and vertical strokes should be properly managed and stretch to the precise point, hence lending the character certain aesthetic appeal.

- **汉代的印章**
  汉代是篆刻发展的高峰时期，印文线条稳健遒劲。
  Seal in the Han Dynasty (206 B.C.-220 A.D.)
  Seal carving has its heyday in the Han Dynasty. The seal impression shows steady and vigorous lines.

- **《兰雪堂》何震（明）**
  何震（约1530—1604），明代著名金石篆刻家，中国古代主流篆刻中徽派篆刻的开山鼻祖。"兰雪堂"为苏州园林拙政园中的一景，此印为朱文印，笔法婀娜刚健，圆劲停匀，颇有小篆遗风。
  He Zhen's Seal of *Orchid Snow Hall* (Ming Dynasty, 1368-1644)
  He Zhen (ca.1530-1604) is a famous metal and stone seal carver of the Ming Dynasty, also known as the founder of Hui school (whose artists mainly came from current Anhui Province), one of the major seal carving schools in ancient China. "Orchid Snow Hall" is a famous scene at the Humble Administrator's Garden in Suzhou. This seal is carved in relief. The knife-work appears robust and energetic, yet also mellow and graceful, retaining a charm of the small seal script.

- 《家在四灵山水间》邓石如（清）

  在秦篆的基础上，邓石如的篆刻融合了金石文字的妙处，形成了"其书由印入，其印由书出"的独特篆法。此印章线条婀娜旖旎，舒展秀丽，表现了作者对故乡山水的情思。

  Deng Shiru's Seven-character Seal of *Dwelling amidst the Landscape* (Qing Dynasty, 1616-1911)

  Deng Shiru's unique seal characters integrate the *Qin* seal script with the merit of metal and stone inscriptions, hence resulting in a perfect combination of the seal carving with calligraphy. The lines of the seal impression stretch with beauty and grace, revealing the craftsman's affection for the landscape of his hometown.

- 《千寻竹斋》吴昌硕（清）

  "斋"简写后，左右两字垂脚均可伸长，且有两边虚处相互呼应之妙，中间两字也密上而疏下，形成一股疏朗空灵之感。

  Wu Changshuo's Four-character Seal of *Room with High Bamboos* (Qing Dynasty, 1616-1911)

  When the character *Zhai* (room) is simplified in form, the neighboring two characters can further stretch their strokes downward. The space left on the right and left sides echoes with each other. The middle two characters are dense in the upper part, sparse in the lower, giving an ethereal air of emptiness.

西泠印社

西泠印社创建于1904年，以"保存金石、研究印学，兼及书画"为宗旨，是中国研究金石篆刻历史最悠久、成就最高、影响最广的学术团体，有"天下第一名社"的盛誉。西泠印社坐落于浙江杭州西湖景区孤山南麓，南至白堤，西近西泠桥，北邻西湖，环境清幽，景色雅致，内建中国印学博物馆。1913年，吴昌硕出任首任社长，弘一法师、黄宾虹、丰子恺等均为西泠印社社员。西泠印社对汉字文化圈内篆刻的创作与发展起到了重要的推动作用。

Xiling Seal Society

Xiling Seal Society was founded in 1904, aiming to "preserve inscribed bronze or stone tablets and study the seal carving as well as seal-related art like calligraphy and painting". It is the oldest and most influential academic community which has also made the most achievements in the study of metal and stone seal carving, hence honored as "the First Seal Society in China". *Xiling* Seal Society is located at the southern foot of Mount Gushan within the scenic area of the West Lake in Hangzhou, Zhejiang Province. The surroundings are quiet, and the scenery is beautiful. To its south stands the Bai Causeway, west is the *Xiling* Bridge and north lies the West Lake. The Seal Study Museum of China is also situated there. In 1913, Wu Changshuo was selected as the first president of the society, while Master Hongyi, Huang Binhong and Feng Zikai were members. *Xiling* Seal Society has played an important role in promoting the creation and development of seal carving in Chinese cultural circle.

- 吴昌硕

吴昌硕（1844—1927）有深厚的书法基础，尤擅篆书。其篆刻风格突破前人而有所创新，艺术成就相当高，受到许多人的盛赞。

Photo of Wu Changshuo

Wu Changshuo (1844-1927) is an expert of calligraphy especially good at seal script. His seal carving breaks the style of all predecessors and finally makes very high artistic achievements which enjoys loud applauds from many sides.

- 黄宾虹

黄宾虹（1865—1955），山水画大师，有"千古以来第一用墨大师"之誉。其篆刻作品虽然不多，但是水平颇高。

Photo of Huang Binhong

Huang Binhong (1865-1955) is a great landscape painter and also revered as "Ink Master of All Ages". His seal sculptures are small in number, but high in quality.

• 弘一法师

弘一法师（1880—1942），俗名李叔同，僧人，中国著名书法家、篆刻家、戏剧家。他成立了继西泠印社之后的"乐石社"，定期整理汇编篆刻方面的资料，为中国篆刻事业做出了突出贡献。

Photo of Master Hongyi

Master Hongyi (1880-1942), Li Shutong, is a Buddhist monk and also a famous Chinese calligrapher, seal carver and dramatist. He founded "the Delight in Stone (*Leshi*) Society" which succeeded the *Xiling* Seal Society. He collected and compiled materials related to seal carving regularly and made great contributions to the cause of Chinese seal carving.

• 丰子恺

丰子恺（1898—1975），中国著名漫画家、散文家。丰子恺师从李叔同学习书画、篆刻等艺术。丰子恺的篆刻作品并不多，但对篆刻却有着深刻的认知。他认为，书画同源，而书实深于画，金石又深于书。

Photo of Feng Zikai

Feng Zikai (1898-1975) is a distinguished Chinese cartoonist and essayist. He learnt painting, calligraphy and seal carving from Li Shutong. Feng Zikai did not leave many seal carvings, but his understanding of seal carving is both deep and thorough. He believes calligraphy and painting share the same origin, but the former is more profound than the latter, whereas metal and stone carving goes even deeper than calligraphy.

- 弘一法师的私人印章（复制版）
  Personal Seal of Master Hongyi (Copy)

- 西泠印社大门
  The Gate of *Xiling* Seal Society

- 西泠印社内景色
  Scenery in *Xiling* Seal Society

印章制作工具

篆刻的印刀，犹如书法的毛笔，是最重要的工具。印刀的粗细、长短、轻重，刀刃的大小、锐钝、平斜都是篆刻者需要考虑的。如何用刀则没有固定的方法，可根据具体情况及个人习惯而定。

印石，是印章的承载者，有玉、石、木、骨、玻璃等多种材料，以柔、脆、腻、坚适中并易于受刀的石质材料为主，其中尤以青田石、寿山石等最为常用。另外，篆刻印章还需要准备临摹书法的毛笔及用于打磨印石的砂纸等辅助工具。

Seal Carving Tools

Knife is to seal carving what writing brush is to calligraphy. The seal carver needs to consider the thickness, length and weight of the knife as well as the size, sharpness and flatness of the carving edge. There is no fixed method to handle the knife. It all depends on the circumstances and personal habits.

• 用于篆刻的印刀
Knife Used in Seal Carving

Seal stone is the substance to bear the impressions. It can vary in materials like jade, stone, wood, bone, glass, etc, among which stones of moderate texture, neither soft nor hard, neither brittle nor greasy, in particular *Qingtian* stone and *Shoushan* stone are most commonly used. Besides, seal carving also needs writing brush to imitate calligraphy, and other auxiliary tools like sandpaper to polish the seal stone.

- 青田石印章

一般印石以青田石最易受刀，青田石产于浙江青田，最名贵的青田石是"封门青"冻石。此印章为清代青田石方章，造型朴实，色彩清新淡雅。

Qingtian Stone Seal

Of all seal stones, *Qingtian* stone is the easiest to cut, *Qingtian* stone is produced in Qingtian County of Zhejiang Province, among which the "*Fengmen* steatite" is the most precious. The seal in the picture is made of *Qingtian* stone in the Qing Dynasty (1616-1911). It is square and plain in shape, fresh and elegant in color.

- 琥珀印章

琥珀是一种石化的天然植物树脂。此印章为清代琥珀椭圆双狮纽章料，晶莹剔透，大小两只狮子造型别致。

Amber Seal

Amber is a kind of natural fossil resin. This amber seal of the Qing Dynasty is oval in shape with two carved lions on the top as button of the seal. It is crystal clear. The big and small lions are creatively molded, hence unique in posture.

- **鸡血石印章**

鸡血石表面红色，像极了鸡血的颜色，故名。同寿山田黄并列，享有"印石皇后"的美称。此印章为清代鸡血石印章，整体以红色为主，圆润光滑，色彩夺目。

Bloodstone Seal

The bloodstone is thus named because of its surface color which is as red as the chicken blood. Together with *Tianhuang* stone, it is revered as "Queen of Seal Stones". This seal is made of bloodstone in the Qing Dynasty. It appears mainly red in color, round and smooth in texture, quite brilliant and eye-catching.

- **田黄印章**

寿山石产于福建寿山，最名贵的是"田黄"，价同黄金。此印章为清代田黄松梅纹章，黄色，半透明。

***Tianhuang* Stone Seal**

Shoushan stone is produced in Shoushan Township, Fujian Province, among which "*Tianhuang* stone" is the most famous and almost as expensive as gold. This seal is made of *Tianhuang* stone in the Qing Dynasty. It has design of pine and plum flower, and is yellow and translucent in color.

章法之美

篆刻的章法，即印面文字的安排和布局，是篆刻的重要组成部分。印章需要在很小的范围内，用不多的文字表现其艺术魅力，不但文字要富有变化，布局更要丰富多彩。篆刻的章法布局需遵循一定的基本原则，包括平稳匀称、挪让呼应、留红空白、盘曲变化、疏密统一、穿插有致以及巧拙适宜等。

平稳匀称是最基本的原则，一

- 《江流有声，断岸千尺》邓石如（清）

此印章法疏密开合，其"疏可走马，密不漏风"的章法安排，体现了险绝有致的审美取向。

Deng Shiru's Eight-character Seal of *Roaring River by High Cliffs* (Qing Dynasty, 1616-1911)

This seal manifests a sharp contrast between density and sparseness in layout. From aesthetic perspective, the composition is abrupt yet quite appealing.

Beauty of Composition

The composition of seal carving, namely the arrangement and layout of characters on the seal surface, constitutes an important part in seal carving. Its aesthetic charm is embodied in the few characters well-organized in limited space. Not only should the characters be varied in form, but the layout needs to be rich and diverse. Normally the layout of seal carving should follow certain basic rules, including balance and symmetry, agreeable position and mutual echoing, fitting blank and red space, proper curve and variation, uniform density, rhythmic insertion as well as good combination of ingenuity and roughness.

Balance and symmetry is the basic principle for seal carving. Generally, characters with multi-strokes should not appear higgledy-piggledy, whereas those with few strokes should not appear sparse. Agreeable position is achieved by moving the strokes of characters to ease the tension of the seal surface. To create mutual echoing, one needs to have symmetric parts on the seal coordinate with each other from afar, such as "echoing between diagonal angles", "opposite sides", "curving strokes", "preserved red space", etc. Proper curve

- 《虚斋》吴昌硕（清）

此作品章法上用中竖将印面分为左右两半，两个字各占一半，保证了每一个字的独立与完美。

Wu Changshuo's Two-Character Seal of *Empty Room* (Qing Dynasty, 1616-1911)

In layout, a vertical line in the middle divides the seal into two parts. Hence either character occupies one half, which ensures the independence and perfection of both in seal carving.

般来讲，要做到笔画多的字不显得繁杂，笔画少的字不显得稀疏。挪让，即通过移动文字笔画的位置来使印面气势舒展；呼应，即使章法上的两个相同部位彼此遥相呼应，一般有"对角呼应""并头呼应""盘曲呼应""留红呼应"等。盘曲变化是为求章法上的协调，对文字做屈伸方圆的处理。印面汉字笔画多寡悬殊的印章，古人通过"疏可走马，密不过针"的方法进行处理，给人以强烈的疏密对比感。穿插有致，是为了打破平板的章法，使字与字相互顾盼，将笔

and variation may further contribute to the balanced layout by manipulating the shape of the characters. For seals with enormous disparity in the number of strokes, the ancients usually enhance the degree of sparsity and density, thus creating a sharp contrastive effect. Rhythmic insertion helps to break the stiff layout and foster the playful relationship between characters by stretching the strokes according to their natural tendency and joining them up. Ingenuity and roughness are two different seal carving styles, which ought to correspond with each other, neither too affected nor too eccentric.

Layout manifests different kinds of spatial relationship and spatial features on the seal surface, including shape, size, density, fantasy vs. reality, proper inclination, distortion and variation, as well as realistic and exaggerating representation. For the sake of layout, sometimes one needs to modify the characters, like to complicate or simplify the character, two characters sharing the same stroke, to stretch, retract or move parts of the character, etc. Besides making adaptations to the structure of the characters, you can also manipulate thickness of the strokes or arrange the

画随势伸缩，上穿下联。巧、拙是两种不同的印章风格，巧拙要适宜，不能太纤媚，也不能太狂怪。

章法在印面上呈现出形状大小、虚实疏密、奇侧均衡、俯仰向背、和谐变形、写实夸张等不同的空间关系与空间特征。出于对印面进行章法布局的需要，有时会对文字加以繁化、简化、共笔、伸缩或移动部位。除了对汉字的结构进行处理外，还可以利用汉字笔画的粗细肥瘦、边框栏格的安排等方式来处理布局。

印章的方寸之地最讲究布白，也就是留出空处。印章的留白处，朱文（印文的两种形式之一，也称"阳文"，指篆刻成凸状的印文）中称"空白"，白文（与朱文framework in order to refine the layout.

Though limited in space, seal carving pays great attention to blank-leaving. Seal characters can be carved in relief (known as red character or "*Yang* character") or in intaglio (known as white character or "*Yin* character"). In the former case, the blank left is called "white space", whereas in the latter, the blank left is called "red space". For ancients, the red and white space is of particular significance. It reflects the artistic principles behind character molding in the layout of seal carving. Moreover, the red and white space is one important method to sharp the contrast of density. We should use it with good flexibility, so the seal impressions will not appear chaotic though dense, nor void because of sparsity.

- 《中国长沙湘潭人也》齐白石（近代）
此印章是齐白石的代表作品，章法恣肆开张，气势夺人而精微不失，表达了画家对故乡的自豪感。

Qi Baishi's Eight-character Seal of *Born in Xiangtan, Changsha, China* (Modern Times)
This seal is Qi Baishi's masterpiece, showing the carver's sense of pride for his hometown. The layout features unrestrained openness, imposing air and also no lack of subtlety.

相对，也称"阴文"，指篆刻成凹状的印文）中称"留红"。古人有"分朱布白"即留红与空白之说，表达了篆刻章法中文字造型美的艺术原理。留红与空白，是篆刻章法中疏密对比最强烈的手段之一，需要灵活处理，做到密而不乱，疏而不空。

大多数印章的字按自上而下、自右向左的顺序进行排列，除此之外，有少数印文顺序为右起横行或回文。有时，为了布局需要，将繁复悬殊的文字斜角对称分布，按照逆时针方向排列，称为"回文"。有时，将单数字排列成双数字以求均衡，或将一简一繁的文字或两个较简单的文字，通过文字部件的置换、重用、省简等方式处理成只占一个字的形式，称为"合文"，又称"合书"。

The characters on most seals are arrayed from top to bottom, from right to left, yet with a few exceptions. Some seal characters always start from the right side and go horizontally. Sometimes for better layout, one may arrange the characters of great disparity in complexity symmetrically across corners and counter-clockwise, which is also known as "*Huiwen*" (backward characters). Sometimes in order to arrange single characters as balanced as double ones, or to make two characters—one simple, one complicated, or both simple in form—occupy the position of one character, one can replace, reuse or omit parts of the characters. This technique is known as "*Hewen*" or "*Heshu*" (combination of characters).

齐白石

齐白石（1864—1957），中国20世纪著名书画大师、篆刻巨匠，世界文化名人。齐白石原名齐璜，别号白石山人，后遂用齐白石之名。他出生于湖南湘潭，晚年定居北京。

齐白石从小为谋生而学习木匠，其后才慢慢走上绘画道路。齐白石年老时改变画法，即"衰年变法"，形成了独特的大写意国画风格，开红花墨叶一派。他擅画瓜果菜蔬花，鸟虫鱼为工绝，兼及人物、山水，与吴昌硕共享"南吴北齐"之誉。戏剧大师梅兰芳（1894—1961）、国画大师李苦禅（1899—1983）等都是齐白石的弟子。

● 齐白石蜡像
Waxen Statue of Qi Baishi

● 齐白石曾用印章
Seals Used by Qi Baishi

Qi Baishi

Qi Baishi (1864-1957) is a distinguished Chinese painter, calligrapher, seal carving master and world cultural celebrity of the 20th century. He was originally named Qi Huang, also known as Baishi Shanren and later began to use the name of Qi Baishi. He was born in Xiangtan, Hunan Province but settled in Beijing in his later years.

Qi Baishi did not take up painting from the very beginning. In childhood he once worked as a carpenter in order to make a living. In senior years, he changed his painting style, started to adopt a unique freehand painting style and also initiated the school of Red Flower with Ink Leaves. He is good at painting fruit, vegetables, flowers, and in particular excels in bird, insect, fish as well as figure and landscape. With Wu Changshuo, they are together honored as "Southern Wu and Northern Qi". Mei Lanfang the dramatic master (1894-1961) and Li Kuchan the remarkable traditional Chinese painter (1899-1983) are all Qi Baishi's disciples.

- 虾图

齐白石作画注重实际观察，他笔下的虾，栩栩如生，活灵活现。

Shrimps

Qi Baishi's paintings rely upon close observation of reality. Shrimps under his brush look almost lifelike in appearance.

> 汉字与诗歌

　　汉字是世界上最有韵律的文字之一，读起来富有节奏感，有一种音乐美。韵律指声韵和节律，是诗词中的平仄格式和押韵规则。古典诗歌这一中国传统文学体裁将汉字的韵律展现得淋漓尽致。历史上有许多著名的诗人，其中唐朝的李白和杜甫两位巨匠最为著名。

　　中国古典诗歌分为古体诗和近体诗两种。古体诗，又叫"古风"，形式自由，较少受格律的束缚，有四言诗、五言诗、七言诗和杂言诗等多种形式。近体诗，又称"今体诗""格律诗"，包括五言律诗、七言律诗和绝句。近体诗出现于唐代初期，有着严格的字数、押韵要求，同时十分注重平仄和对仗。近体诗讲究格律，节奏

> Chinese Characters and Poetry

Chinese is one of the most rhythmic languages in the world and reads with a musical cadence. Rhythm refers to sound and rhyme, i.e. the *Ping* and *Ze* pattern (level and oblique tones) and the rhyming rules. Classical poetry, traditional Chinese literary genre, fully demonstrates the rhythmic beauty of Chinese characters. There are many famous poets in Chinese history, among which Li Bai and Du Fu of the Tang Dynasty are the most distinguished.

　　Classical Chinese poetry can be divided into archaic group and modern group. Archaic poetry, also known as archaic style, is free in form, seldom restricted by rules like tonal pattern or rhyme scheme. It usually has four, five or seven characters in a line or diverse number of characters in different lines.

李白、杜甫
Li Bai and Du Fu

　　李白（701—762），中国伟大的浪漫主义诗人，被后人尊为"诗仙"。存世诗文千余篇，代表作有《静夜思》《望庐山瀑布》《蜀道难》《将进酒》等诗篇，有《李太白集》传世。李白的诗歌创作带有强烈的主观色彩，侧重抒写豪迈气概和激昂情怀，且想象奇特。李白的诗雄奇飘逸，颇有"笔落惊风雨，诗成泣鬼神"之势，艺术成就极高。他讴歌祖国山河与自然风光，风格奔放，俊逸清新，富有浪漫主义色彩，达到了内容与形式的完美统一。

Li Bai (701-762) is a great Chinese romantic poet revered as "Poet Immortal" by later generations. He has left us more than one thousand poems, among which masterpieces include *Thoughts in the Quiet Night*, *View of Waterfall at Mount Lushan*, *Difficulty of the Road to Shu*, *Beginning in the Wine*, etc. It is really fortunate that *Collected Poetry of Li Taibai* has been handed down from ancient times. His verse shows strong subjective color, full of heroic spirit

● 李白画像
李白平生嗜酒，喜爱游山玩水，个性洒脱，追求无拘无束的生活。
Portrait of Li Bai
Li Bai is addicted to drinking all lifetime. He is also fond of traveling among the landscape. Ardent and obstinate, he pursues a carefree and unfettered life.

and fierce passion, also rich with imagination and variation. Indeed, his poetry is of high artistic achievements, giving a magnificent and elegant air, with a momentum that can stun the wind and rain and drive the ghosts into tears. He celebrates landscape of the motherland and the natural scenery in a bold and unrestrained manner. The fresh and elegant style is tinted with strong romantic color and reveals perfect unity between content and artistic form.

诗文 · Poetry

《望庐山瀑布之二》
李白（唐）

日照香炉生紫烟，
遥看瀑布挂前川。
飞流直下三千尺，
疑是银河落九天。

View of Waterfall at Mount Lushan II

by Li Bai (Tang Dynasty, 618-907)

Sunlit is the Incense Summit, aglow in smoke and steam;
To afar like a shimmering curtain, a waterfall hangs upstream—
Flowing, flying, fluttering, plunging three thousand feet,
As if it was the Silver River, falling from the Heaven Supreme.

这是李白初游庐山时所作的两首诗之一。另一首为五言古诗，这首为七言绝句。

When first travelling to Mount Lushan, Li Bai composed two poems on the way: one is five-character old-style verse (free in meter, rhyme and number of lines), the other is seven-character four-line verse.

诗文 · Poetry

《静夜思》
李白（唐）

床前明月光，
疑是地上霜。
举头望明月，
低头思故乡。

Thoughts in the Quiet Night
by Li Bai (Tang Dynasty, 618-907)

A bed, I see a silver light;
I wonder if it's frost aground.
Looking up, I find the moon bright;
Bowing, in homesickness I'm drowned.

李白表达思乡之情的名作，在中国可谓妇孺皆知。

This poem is Li Bai's representative work that expresses homesickness and quite popular in China.

杜甫（712—770），唐代伟大的现实主义诗人，被后世尊为"诗圣"，与李白合称"李杜"。由于其诗以忧虑国家存亡、同情老百姓的困苦等现实主义题材为主，被称为"诗史"。《新安吏》《石壕吏》《潼关吏》《新婚别》《垂老别》《无家别》《春望》《绝句》《望岳》等都是杜甫脍炙人口的作品，有《杜工部集》传世。杜甫的作品以古体、律诗见长，其诗风沉郁顿挫。

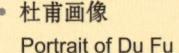 杜甫画像
Portrait of Du Fu

Du Fu (712-770) is a great realist poet of the Tang Dynasty later revered as "Poet Sage". Along with Li Bai, they are collectedly known as "Li and Du". As his poems mainly center upon realistic themes, like the fate of the country or the suffering common people, his poems are also referred to as "Poet Historian". Du Fu's popular poems include *Recruiting Officer at Xin'an, Recruiting Officer at Shihao, Recruiting Officer at Tongguan, Newlywed's Departure, Old Couple's Departure, Homeless Man's Departure, Spring View, Quatrain, Gazing at the Mountain*, etc. *The Collected Poems of Du Fu* has been handed down for generations. His poems are mostly in old and regulated style, tinted with a color of melancholy and frustration.

诗文 · Poetry

《登高》
杜甫（唐）

风急天高猿啸哀，渚清沙白鸟飞回。
无边落木萧萧下，不尽长江滚滚来。
万里悲秋常作客，百年多病独登台。
艰难苦恨繁霜鬓，潦倒新停浊酒杯。

On the Height

by Du Fu (Tang Dynasty, 618-907)

The wind so swift, the sky so wide, apes wail and cry;
Water so clear and beach so white, birds wheel and fly.
The boundless forest sheds its leaves shower by shower;
The endless river rolls its waves hour after hour.
A thousand miles from home, I'm grieved at autumn's plight;
Ill now and then for years, alone I'm on this height.
Living in times so hard, at frosted hair I pine;
Cast down by poverty, I have to give up wine.

杜甫晚年生活潦倒，此诗作于767年，是其病卧夔州时所写。
In his later years Du Fu lead quite a hard life. This poem is composed at Kuizhou in 767 A.D. when he was ill in bed.

诗文 · Poetry

《绝句》
杜甫（唐）

两个黄鹂鸣翠柳，
一行白鹭上青天。
窗含西岭千秋雪，
门泊东吴万里船。

Quatrain
by Du Fu (Tang Dynasty, 618-907)

Two golden orioles sing amid the willows green;
A row of white egrets fly into the blue sky.
From my window the snow-crowned western hills are seen;
Beyond the door the east-bound ships at anchor lie.

绝句每首四句，有五言绝句和七言绝句两种。

Quatrain is a poem of four lines. Each line has five or seven characters.

鲜明，读起来铿锵有力、抑扬顿挫，富有美感，在中国诗歌史上有着重要地位。在近体诗中，汉字的韵律美通过平仄与押韵得到充分体现。

平仄

平指平直，仄指曲折，平声、仄声交替使用，就能够产生声调上抑扬顿挫的节奏感。中国汉字的古代声调与现在声调有所不同，古代汉字的声调有四声，分别为平声、上声、去声、入声，其中入声在现代用普通话注音的汉字中已经消失。平声即为平声，上声、去声、入声属于仄声。按传统的说法，平声是平调，上声是升调，去声是降调，入声是短调。

绝句，是近体诗的一种常见类型，有严格的格律要求。绝句每首四句，通常分五言绝句和七言绝句两种，简称"五绝""七绝"。绝句起源于汉代，成形于魏晋南北朝，兴盛于唐朝。唐宋是中国诗词最为繁荣的时期，绝句名作层出不穷。

五言绝句的平仄格式以仄起为

Modern poetry, also known as modern style or metrical poetry, includes five-character eight-line verse, seven-character eight-line verse and four-line verse. Modern poetry first appeared in the early Tang Dynasty, characterized by a strict number of characters, rhyming regulation, particular tonal pattern and antithesis. Modern poetry is also particular about meters and demands distinct rhymes that read sonorous, melodious and rich in beauty. Briefly, it occupies an important position in the history of Chinese poetry and in modern poetry, the metrical beauty of Chinese characters can be fully demonstrated through the tonal pattern and rhymes.

Ping and *Ze* Pattern (Level and Oblique Tones)

Ping means level, whereas *Ze* means oblique. Alternating use of *Ping* and *Ze* tones will produce melodious intonation. The ancient tones of Chinese characters are a bit different from those of modern ones. In ancient phonetics, a Chinese character usually has four tones, respectively level tone, rising, falling and entering tone, among which the entering tone has disappeared in modern phonetic system. *Ping* refers exclusively to the

常见，盛唐诗人王之涣（688—742）登高望远时所写的五言绝句《登鹳雀楼》，即为仄起式。

全诗原文如下：

白日依山尽，
Bái rì yī shān jìn,
黄河入海流。
huáng hé rù hǎi liú。
欲穷千里目，
Yù qióng qiān lǐ mù,
更上一层楼。
gèng shàng yī céng lóu。

按照唐代人的读音，这首《登鹳雀楼》的平仄声调为：
仄仄平平仄，
平平仄仄平。
（平）平平仄仄，
仄仄仄平平。
注：括号里为可平、可仄。

全诗的意思是：夕阳依傍着西山慢慢地沉没，滔滔黄河朝着东海汹涌奔流。若想把千里的风光景物看够，那就得登上更高一层的城楼。

level tone, whereas the other three are collected known as Ze. In traditional conception, the first three tones, just as their name suggested, sound respectively even, rising and falling. The entering tone turns out quite short.

Quatrain is a common genre in modern poetry that adheres to strict metrical rules. It has four lines, each line consisting of five or seven characters. Hence the quatrain can divide into "five-character quatrain" and "seven-character quatrain". The Chinese quatrain was originated in the Han Dynasty (206 B.C.-220 A.D.), matured during the Wei, Western Jin, Eastern Jin and Southern and Northern dynasties (220-589), and flourished in the Tang Dynasty (618-907). In fact, the Tang and Song dynasties (618-1279) witnessed the heyday of Chinese poetry when masterpieces of quatrain sprang up endlessly.

In terms of tonal pattern, five-character quatrains usually begin with *Ze* tones. The ambitious quatrain *On the Stork Tower* is a typical example. It is written by Wang Zhihuan (688-742), a great poet in the glorious period of the Tang Dynasty, when ascending a height to view the distance. A phonetic view of the verse is given below:

押韵

押韵，就是把具有相同韵母的字放在规定的位置上，使朗诵或咏唱诗歌时，产生铿锵的和谐感。近体诗为了使声调和谐、容易记忆，十分讲究押韵。

孟浩然（689—740）隐居在鹿门山时所作的五言绝句《春晓》，全诗表达了诗人对春天的热爱和怜惜之情，韵脚在第一、第二、第四

- **孟浩然画像**

孟浩然，唐代著名山水田园派代表诗人，其诗作以五言为主，多写山水田园和隐居的逸兴以及羁旅行役的心情。

Portrait of Meng Haoran

Meng Haoran (689-740) is a famous landscape and pastoral poet of the Tang Dynasty. Most of his verses are short five-character quatrains that celebrate landscape and pastoral beauty, betraying delight in seclusion as well as joy in travelling.

Bái rì yī shān jìn, huáng hé rù hǎi liú.
Yù qióng qiān lǐ mù, gèng shàng yī céng lóu.

The *Ping* (signified by "--") and *Ze* (signified by "V") tones of this five-character poem fit neatly into this pattern:

V V -- -- V, -- -- V V --.
(--) -- -- V V, V V V -- --.

Note that the brackets mean the character can be either level or oblique in tones.

The general meaning of this poem goes, "The sun slowly sinks behind the western hills, and toward the Eastern Sea the surging Yellow River roars. Wish you an endless view to cheer your eyes? Then one more story mount and higher rise."

Rhyme

Rhyme is created by putting characters of the same vowel at the given position. Thus when reciting or chanting, the poem will sound sonorous and harmonious. In order to bring tones into consonance and also facilitate memorization, modern poetry pays particular attention to rhymes.

When Meng Haoran (689-740) lived in seclusion at Mount Lumen, he

优美的汉字 The Graceful Chinese Character

句，分别为"晓""鸟""少"，押ao韵。

全诗原文如下：

春眠不觉晓，
Chūn mián bù jué xiǎo,
处处闻啼鸟。
chù chù wén tí niǎo。
夜来风雨声，
Yè lái fēng yǔ shēng,
花落知多少。
huā luò zhī duō shǎo。

全诗的意思是：春日酣梦不知不觉到了早晨，到处都是鸟儿明快的啼叫声。想起夜里的那阵阵风雨声，感叹不知道有多少花儿零落。

wrote the famous five-character quatrain named *Spring Dawn*. Through the poem, the speaker conveys his love and pity for spring. Three characters at the end of the first, second and fourth lines mutually rhyme with each other. They are respectively *Xiao* (dawn), *Niao* (bird) and *Shao* (little), all containing the vowel "ao". A phonetic view of the verse is given below:

Chūn mián bù jué xiǎo, chù chù wén tí niǎo.

Yè lái fēng y ǔ shēng, huā luò zhī duō shǎo.

The meaning of the poem goes, "Sleeping not knowing it's morning. Birds are singing lively here and there. Thinking of the rain and wind at night, I wonder how many flowers are fallen there."

＞ 汉字与对联

对联，又称"楹联"，俗称"对子"，是一种独特的汉字艺术形式，分为诗对联和散文对联，相传为后蜀（934—965）的末代皇帝孟昶（chǎng）（919—965）所创。对联起源于桃符，桃符是古代人挂在门上的刻有或画有门神图像、名字的桃木板。古人相信，桃木可以驱灾辟邪。对联一般写在纸、布或者刻在竹子、柱子上，是一种对偶文学，讲究内容相连、对仗工整以及平仄协调。

对联在韵律上的要求与诗歌相似，但是也有讲求自由不遵循韵律标准而创作的对联。对联格律概括起来有六大要素，又叫"六相"：一是汉字的字数要相等，即上联字数等于下联字数；二是汉字的词性

＞ Chinese Characters and Chinese Couplet

Chinese couplet, also known as couplet hung on columns of the hall, is commonly referred to as the "pair". As a unique art form of Chinese characters, it can be divided into poetic couplet and prosaic couplet. According to legend, it was created by Meng Chang (919-965), the last emperor of the Later Shu State (934-965). Couplets are originally peach wood charms carved or painted with door-god and name, then hung on the gate by the ancients to ward off evil and disaster. Couplets are generally written on paper and cloth, or carved on bamboos and columns. It is a pair of corresponding lines related in content, neat in antithesis and coordinate in tonal pattern.

Similar to poetry, Chinese couplet also follows strict metrical rules. However, there are exceptions where

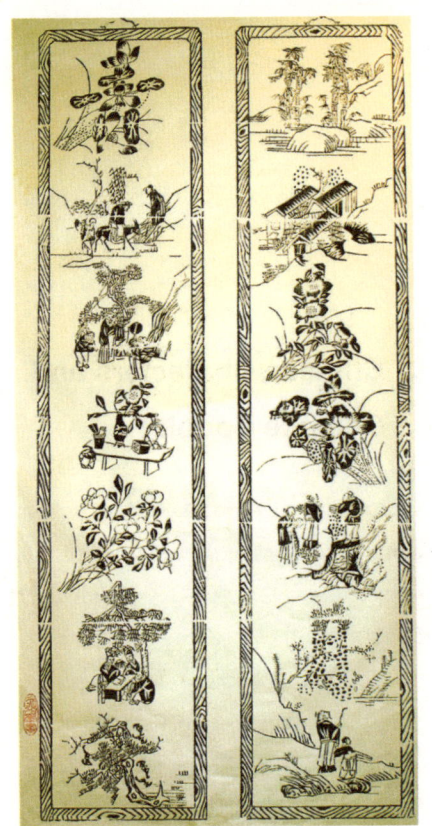

● 竹林对联年画（明）

New Year Painting with Couplet and Bamboo Grove (Ming Dynasty, 1368-1644)

the writer stresses freedom in creation and hence does not go by the standard form. Generally, a regular couplet should adhere to six rules, also known as *Liuxiang* (six sameness). First, both lines should have the same number of Chinese characters. Second, the lexical category of each character must be the same as or similar to that of its corresponding character. Third, the structure of phrase and sentence should be as identical as possible in the two lines. Fourth, corresponding rhythm, i.e. two lines should pause at the same place. Fifth, harmonious *Ping* and *Ze*, that is, the tonal pattern in a specific position of one line must be the inverse of the other. Lastly, the meaning of the two lines needs to be related, just as the term "couplet" suggests. When you meet all these requirements, the couplet will not only turn out sonorous and catchy but read extremely melodious.

Gu Xiancheng (1550-1612), the great thinker of the Ming Dynasty once inscribed a couplet for *Donglin* Academy to admonish the scholars who should not only devote to academic studies, but care about worldly affairs instead of being bookworms. The couplet can be literally translated as follows. A phonetic view of

相当，即上下联同一位置的词或词组应具有相同或相近词性；三是结构相称，即上下联语句的词组和句式之结构应当尽可能相同；四是节奏相应，即上下联停顿的地方必须一致；五是平仄相谐，上下联之间特定位置的字平仄要相反；六是内容相关，对联的"联"就是指上下联之间的内容相关。以上诸多要求，使得对联阅读起来朗朗上口，节奏起伏变化，具有韵律美。

明代思想家顾宪成（1550—1612）为其创办的江苏无锡东林书院题写了一副对联，告诫读书人不仅要读好书，还要关心天下之事，而不要读死书。

风声雨声读书声，声声入耳；
Fēng shēng yǔ shēng dú shū shēng, shēng shēng rù ěr;
家事国事天下事，事事关心。
Jiā shì guó shì tiān xià shì, shì shì guān xīn。

此联中上下两联的字数相等：上、下联各11个字。两联对应位置的汉字词性相当：上联中的三个名词"风声""雨声""读书声"分别对应下联中的三个名词"家事""国事""天下事"。同时，上联的"声声入耳"与下联的"事事关心"，这两个词组的词性也相同。此联的结构对称：上联中的"风声"对"家事"，"雨声"对

the couplet is also given below.

Sounds of wind, rain and reading are close to the ears,
Affairs of home, state and world are deep in the heart.

Fēng shēng yǔ shēng dú shū shēng, shēng shēng rù ěr;
Jiā shì guó shì tiān xià shì, shì shì guān xīn.

In this couplet, each line has eleven characters which are also corresponding in part of speech. To be specific, there are three nouns in the first line, respectively "wind, rain and reading", corresponding with the three nouns in the second line, "home, state and world". Meanwhile, "close to the ears" and "deep in the heart" also belong to the same lexical category. This couplet is also symmetrical in structure. Terms and phrases of the first line match with those of the second line in character numbers. Moreover, two lines are coordinate in rhythm, pausing at the same places: The sounds of wind / rain / and reading / are close to the ears; the affairs of home / state / and world / are deep in the heart. *Ping* and *Ze* of the couplet also go by the tonal pattern "-- -- V -- V -- --, -- -- V V; V V -- V -- V V, V

"国事","读书声"对"天下事","声声入耳"对"事事关心",分别是两个字对两个字、三个字对三个字、四个字对四个字,上下结构对称。此联的节奏相应:上、下联的停顿为"风声/雨声/读书声/声声入耳,家事/国事/天下事/事事关心",互相对应。此联的平仄相谐,富有音律:平平仄平仄平平,平平仄仄;仄仄平仄平仄仄,仄仄平平。此联的内容相互关联:由学堂内外的各种声音,关联家庭

V -- --", which is full of melody. Besides, the content of the first line is related with that of the second line. The writer draws a comparison between various sounds inside or outside the school and various worldly affairs to make a point that one should keep patriotism or national well-being in mind when pursuing academic studies. It is both of high ideological level and artistic quality.

Couplet pasting is a traditional custom of China. People can write couplets all by themselves or buy ready-

• 江苏无锡东林书院
Donglin Academy at Wuxi, Jiangsu Province

- 东林书院依庸堂
Yiyong Hall at Donglin Academy

内外的各种事件，强调了读书不忘忧国的爱国主义思想，既有很强的思想性，又有极高的艺术性。

贴对联是中国传统习俗，人们可以自己泼墨挥毫自做对联，也可以上街购买对联，将其贴在大门上。红色的对联将宅院装点一新，代表了人们祈求幸福、平安的美好愿望。每当春节，家家户户都会在大门上张贴红火的对联，这其中就不乏经典妙对。

made ones on the street. When pasted on the gate, the red couplets not only help adorn the house, but express one's best wishes for peace and happiness. Whenever the Spring Festival falls, every household will post red couplets on the gate of the courtyard, among which there is no lack of classic pieces. For instance:

Moral integrity like honesty and kindness gives the family eternal prosperity;

Fine education of reading and

忠厚传家久，

Zhōng hòu chuán jiā jiǔ,

诗书继世长。

Shī shū jì shì cháng.

这副对联上下联各5个字。"忠厚"与"诗书"相对，"传家久"与"继世长"相对，达到了词性相当、结构对称的要求。其节奏为忠厚/传家久，诗书/继世长。此联的平仄音律为：平仄平平仄，平平仄仄平，符合平仄对称的要求。此联是朗朗上口、音韵和谐的佳作。

writing ensures the nation perpetual development.

Zhōng hòu / chuan jiā jiǔ ;
Shī shū / jì shì cháng.

In this couplet, each line has five Chinese characters. "Honesty and kindness" corresponds with "reading and writing" in part of speech, whereas "gives the family eternal prosperity" matches with "ensures the nation perpetual development" in structure. With respect to rhythm, both lines are paused only one time behind their subjects. The *Ping* and *Ze* pattern goes as "-- V -- -- V, -- -- V V --" which is symmetrical and reads quite catchy and sounds fairly harmonious.

- **北京四合院大门上的对联**（图片提供：全景正片）
此联的意思是：保持忠义厚道的品德才能让家族长盛不衰，注重读书教育才能让民族长远发展。
Couplet Posted on the Gate of Beijing Courtyard
The meaning of the couplet can be translated as, "Moral integrity like honesty and kindness gives the family eternal prosperity, whereas fine education of reading and writing ensures the nation perpetual development."

古今第一长联

　　云南昆明滇池大观楼上有一副长达180字的对联,是中国最为著名的一副长联,有"古今第一长联"的美誉。作者为被后人尊称为"联圣"的清朝乾隆年间诗人、文学家孙髯翁,此联为其登大观楼时有感而作。

　　上联:

　　五百里滇池,奔来眼底。披襟岸帻,喜茫茫空阔无边。看:东骧神骏,西翥灵仪,北走蜿蜒,南翔缟素。高人韵士,何妨选胜登临。趁蟹屿螺洲,梳裹就风鬟雾鬓。更蘋天苇地,点缀些翠羽丹霞。莫辜负:四周香稻,万顷晴沙,九夏芙蓉,三春杨柳。

● 云南昆明滇池大观楼（图片提供：全景正片）
Grand View Pavilion at Dian Lake in Kunming, Yunnan Province

下联：

　　数千年往事，注到心头。把酒凌虚，叹滚滚英雄何在。想：汉习楼船，唐标铁柱，宋挥玉斧，元跨革囊。伟烈丰功，费尽移山心力。尽珠帘画栋，卷不及暮雨朝云。便断碣残碑，都付与苍烟落照。只赢得：几杵疏钟，半江渔火，两行秋雁，一枕清霜。

The Longest Couplet Ever Existent

The couplet on the Grand View Pavilion at Dian Lake of Kunming, Yunnan Province is known as "the longest couplet ever existed in China" with 180 characters. It was composed by Sun Ranweng when he felt so touched at the Grand View Pavilion. Sun is a great poet and man of letters in the Qianlong Period of the Qing Dynasty (1736-1795) and revered as "Couplet Sage" by later generations.

　　The first part of the couplet talks highly of the various scenic areas of Kunming and the breathtaking views they afford. The Dian Lake stretches hundreds of miles, vast and boundless. To survey all around, east, west, south and north all present magnificence, as if inviting refined noblemen to have a dose of their beauty. When wind and mist frequent the wavy hills, rays of sunshine entertain themselves amidst the emerald groves. What about a bath in the fragrant rice flowers? With dripping charm, the summer lotus and spring willows may definitely drive you into tears of joy.

　　The second half of the couplet gives an insight into Yunnan's history, spanning thousands of years and concludes that no matter how big a battle is won, everything, including the glory earned from such battles, yields to nothingness in the end. When drinking, one cannot help to deplore the fate of heroes. Indeed throughout history, great feats are achieved at too much expense. At last, all seems so inferior and void compared with the natural beauty.

附录
Appendix

> 汉字书写工具

现存最早的汉字"甲骨文"是先人用刀刻在龟甲、兽骨上的。其实汉字的书写载体很多，由金属、竹简、木牍、绢帛到如今的纸张等。龟甲、兽骨只用于记录占卜结果，属于用途专一的特殊书写材料。书写工具也从刀演变成动物毛制成的毛笔，随着科技的发展，更是出现了高科技的电脑输入等新型书写方式。

文房四宝，是中国传统书法创作的主要用具，也是古代汉字的主要书写工具。文房四宝，分别指笔、墨、纸、砚，因其放在书房之中使用（文房即书房），因而被称为"文房四宝"。这一称呼起源于南北朝时期，历史上，"文房四宝"所指之物屡有变化。自宋朝以

> Writing Tools of Chinese Characters

The earliest Chinese characters, i.e. oracle-bone inscriptions were carved by the primitives on animal bones. Materials like metal, bamboo, gold foil, silk and modern paper only emerge gradually in later times. By and by, brush made of animal hairs replaced knife as the writing tool. Now with the development of science and technology, new writing styles like computer input also come into being.

The Four Treasures of the Study are major writing tools applied in traditional Chinese calligraphy. They are respectively writing brush, ink, paper and inkstone, which are commonly referred to as "Four Treasures of the Study" because they are mainly used there. This form of address originates in the Southern and Northern dynasties (420-589) but refers

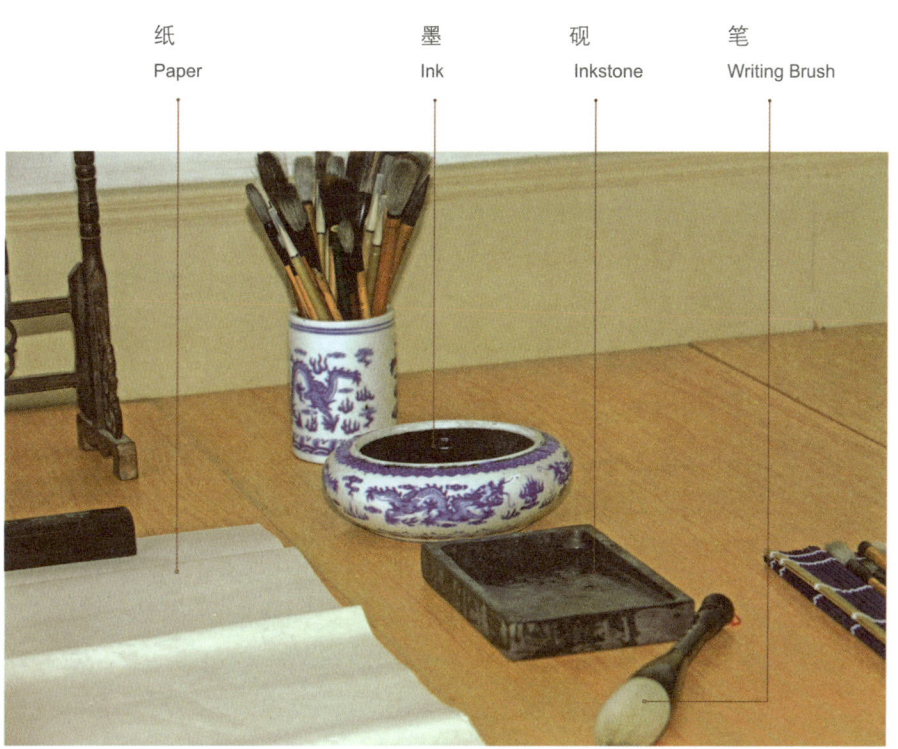

纸 Paper　墨 Ink　砚 Inkstone　笔 Writing Brush

• 文房四宝
Four Treasures of the Study

来，"文房四宝"特指浙江湖州的湖笔、安徽徽州的徽墨、安徽泾县的宣纸、广东肇庆的端砚。

笔，即毛笔，是中国的传统书写工具，由竹子制成的筒杆和动物毛做成的笔头组成。毛笔产生于新石器时代，先人使用毛笔描绘彩陶纹饰。依笔毛弹性的强弱，毛笔可分为软毫、硬毫、兼毫等。

to different objects in different historical periods. Since the Northern Song and Southern Song dynasties (960-1279), the "Four Treasures" specifically refer to writing brush produced at Huzhou, Zhejiang Province, ink produced at Huizhou, Anhui Province, rice paper made in Jing County, Anhui Province, and inkstone made in Zhaoqing, Guangdong Province.

Writing brush is a traditional writing

选择毛笔，需要注意四点：笔毫的末端要尖锐，毫尖要平齐，毫毛要充足，笔腰要有弹性。河北衡水的侯笔、安徽宣城的宣笔和浙江湖州的湖笔是中国最为著名的三种毛笔。

墨，即黑墨，是古代书写必不可少的文房用具。墨既包括古代文人书写、绘画时使用的黑色颜料，也包括朱墨和其他各种彩色墨汁。按用途划分，墨还可以分为用来书写的松烟墨和用来作画的油烟墨两种。

史前有文饰的彩陶、商周刻有文字的甲骨以及后来有文字或绘画

instrument originated in China. The shaft of the brush is made of bamboo, whereas the head is made of animal hairs. It first appeared in the Neolithic Age (ca. 8000 years ago) when the primitives used it to portray patterns on painted potteries. Based on the elasticity of the hairs, writing brush can be divided into three categories, soft-haired, hard-haired, and soft-hard combined brush.

When selecting writing brush, one should particularly pay attention to four aspects: a. the end of the brush hairs should be pointed; b. the tip should be level; c. the hairs should be adequate; d. the waist of the brush should be elastic. *Hou* Brush made in Hengshui,

笔尖　　笔毫　　　　　　笔杆
Brush Tip　Brush Hair　　Brush Shaft

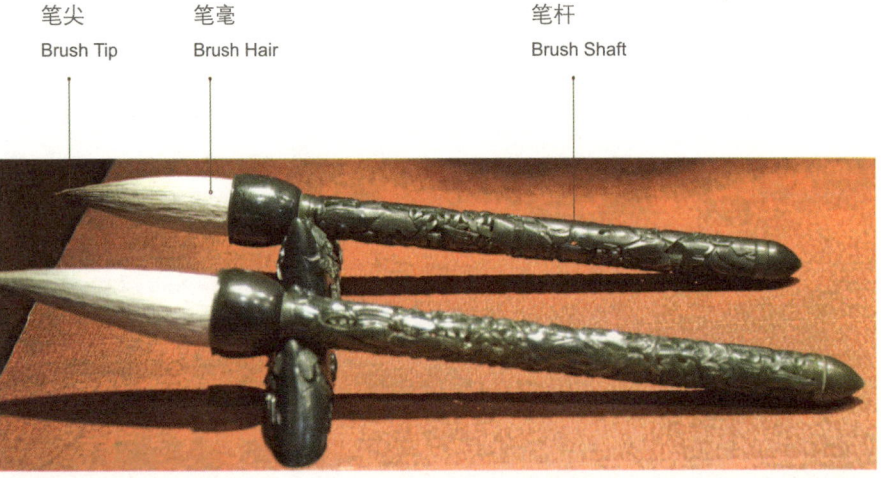

• 毛笔
Writing Brush

- 毛笔装饰

汉代时，人们就已经开始在笔杆上刻字、镶饰。

Decoration of Writing Brush

As early as the Han Dynasty (206 B.C.-220 A.D.), people had already begun to decorate brush shafts with inscription or other design.

的竹简、木牍、缣帛等物品上都可以看到原始用墨的痕迹。陶工制器、卜师占卜中也曾使用墨。秦代以前，古人磨石炭成汁制成墨，称为"石墨"。秦汉时，开始出现人工

Hebei Province, *Xuan* Brush produced in Xuancheng, Anhui Province, and *Hu* Brush made in Huzhou, Zhejiang Province are so far the most famous writing brushes in China.

Ink, or black ink is one essential study tool for ancient writing. It can be the black pigment used by ancient literati in painting and calligraphy, or ink made of vermilion and other colored pigments. In terms of usage, ink can divide into two groups, pine-soot ink for calligraphy and lampblack ink for painting.

Ancient use of ink can be traced from the patterns on prehistoric painted potteries as well as the oracle-bone inscriptions, bamboo slip, silk calligraphy and painting in the Shang Dynasty, Western Zhou Dynasty and Eastern Zhou Dynasty (1600 B.C.-256 B.C.). People also used ink in woodwork and divination. Before the Qin Dynasty (221 B.C.-206 B.C.), the ancients made ink by grinding coal and called it stone ink. During the Qin and Han dynasties (221 B.C.-220 A.D.), artificial ink emerged which was made from pine soot, tune coal and rubber. *Qimin Yaoshu* (literally *Main Techniques for the Welfare of the People*) written by Jia Sixie of the Northern Wei Dynasty (386-534) has the earliest account of the method of ink making.

墨，原料为松烟、桐煤、胶等。北魏（386—534）贾思勰的《齐民要术》是最早记述制墨方法的著作。

书法的笔法与墨法同样重要。浓墨是最主要的一种墨法，书写时行笔实而沉，具有凝重沉稳、神采外耀的效果。使用墨时，需要加入清水研磨，加水不宜过多，且水中不能混有杂质，磨墨时要用力均

In calligraphy, ink is as equally important as the movement of strokes. Thick ink is a most popular method of writing whereby the brush moves steadily to produce an expressive and dazzling effect. To have ink, one needs to grind the inkstone with adequate amount of clear water that has no impurities. When grinding, you should give even strength and rub slowly till the ink appears thick.

● 墨

墨有方形、圆形、不规则形状等不同造型。在书写、绘画时，用墨富有感情，能力透纸背，入木三分。

Ink Stick

Ink stick can be square, round or irregular in shape. In calligraphy or painting, only when the use of ink involves enough sentiments can the work be forceful and profound.

- **宣纸**

  宣纸原产于安徽泾县，起源于唐代。宣纸因其良好的润墨性、耐久性、柔韧性和抗虫性而被广泛用来绘画和写字。

  Rice Paper

  Rice paper, originated in the Tang Dynasty (618-907), was first produced in Jing County, Anhui Province. Because of its fine absorbency, durability, flexibility and insect-resistance, rice paper is widely used in painting and writing.

匀，慢慢地研磨，直到墨汁浓稠。

纸，即宣纸，是供毛笔书写或画画用的独特的手工纸，质地柔韧、洁白平滑、色泽耐久、吸水力强。造纸术是中国的四大发明之一，秦汉时期，古人已经学会使用树皮、破布等原料制造纸，但是当时的纸张质地粗糙，不便于书写。唐代以后，造纸技术得到提升，宣纸出现。书法讲究用纸，不同的纸

Paper, or rice paper, is a handmade material specifically used in Chinese calligraphy and painting. It is soft and smooth in texture, white and durable in color, and also quite absorbent. Papermaking is one of China's four great inventions. Early in the Qin and Han dynasties (221 B.C.-220 A.D.), the ancients began to use bark, rags and other materials to make paper. It is obvious that paper thus produced was rough in texture and not easy to write. After the Tang Dynasty (618-907), as the papermaking technique got improved, rice paper came into being. Calligraphy is quite particular about the quality of paper. In practice, different kinds of paper are suitable for different writing styles.

Inkstone, is a tool used to grind pigments in calligraphy and painting, hence hailed as "Foremost of the Four Treasures" by the ancients. Inkstones are mostly made of stone, but we can also

- **蔡伦造纸**

  东汉蔡伦（61—121）改进了传统的造纸技术，使用树皮、渔网等原料，运用挫、捣、抄、烘等工艺制造纸，这种纸因此被称为"蔡侯纸"。

  Cai Lun and Papermaking

  In the Eastern Han Dynasty, Cai Lun (61-121) improved the traditional papermaking technology. He used bark and fishnet as materials, and then by a series of craftwork like pressing, pounding, copying, drying, etc. made the paper now known as the "Caihou Paper".

类有不同的用处，适合创作不同风格的作品。

砚，即砚台。砚台，是书写、绘画研磨色料的工具，被古人誉为"文房四宝之首"。砚台有玉、漆、瓷、石等多种材质，其中以石质最为普遍。砚台讲究质地细腻、润泽净纯、晶莹平滑、纹理色秀、易发墨而不吸水。许多砚台因其艺术性的外观和细腻的质地而成为人们的收藏品。书法讲究用砚，砚台

see other materials like jade, lacquer, porcelain, etc. A good inkstone should be delicate, moist, smooth, translucent and fine-grained in texture, easy to produce ink and non-absorbent. Many inkstones gradually become people's collections because of their artistic appearance and delicate texture. Calligraphy is very particular about inkstones. One should clean the inkstone everyday with clear water, so that it can be renewed in quality.

In addition to such traditional

- 砚台

汉代时砚已流行，宋代时被普遍使用，明、清两代品种繁多，出现了被人们称为"四大名砚"的端砚、歙砚、洮砚和澄泥砚。

Inkstone

Early in the Han Dynasty (206 B.C.-220 A.D.), inkstone became the fashion. When it came to the Song Dynasty (960-1279), inkstone came into common use. Towards the Ming and Qing dynasties (1368-1911), different varieties of inkstone emerged, including the well-known "Four Famous Inkstones", respectively *Duan* Inkstone produced in Duanxi, Guangdong Province, *She* Inkstone made in She County, Anhui Province, *Tao* Inkstone in Gansu Province, and *Chengni* Inkstone from Luoyang, Henan Province.

- 书写常用工具——钢笔
  Common Writing Tool—
  Fountain Pen

必须坚持每天换水清洗，方能常用常新。

除了毛笔、墨汁、宣纸、砚台等传统书写工具，在如今的日常生活中，汉字主要由钢笔等硬笔书写，并随之出现硬笔书法。硬笔书法与软笔（毛笔）书法的原理大致相同，但是由于两者的笔头一个为细且硬的金属笔尖，一个为粗且软的兽毛笔尖，因此写出的汉字具有不一样的美感。

人们使用钢笔、圆珠笔等书写，将信息记录在各种纸张上。现代书籍上的汉字，则是通过印刷技术形成的铅字。随着现代科技的发展，汉字的书写也已经电子化了。

writing tools as brush, ink, rice paper and inkstone, now people mainly use fountain pen to write Chinese characters, which gradually results in pen calligraphy. Pen calligraphy follows similar theoretical rules as brush calligraphy, but since the former features thin and hard metal tip, the latter thick and soft plumy tip, the characters they produce usually carry beauty of different kinds.

People use fountain pens and ballpoint pens to record information on a variety of paper. But characters on modern books are all movable types formed by printing technology. Moreover, with the development of modern technology, the writing of Chinese characters also reveals an electronic trend.

> 如何写汉字

写字是了解汉字的一个重要方法，也是表现自我的一种重要方式。学习写字并不是一件容易的事，书写者要有写好字的信心，不气馁，保持耐性。从使用工具来说，依据个人的喜好，使用钢笔、圆珠笔、铅笔都可以，这里以钢笔书写为例进行说明。

首先，书写姿势要正确。这是写好字的前提，同时还可以保护视力，减少疲劳。一般来说，书写者要做到头部端正略向前倾斜，身子直挺，双臂打开平放在桌面上，两脚自然分开平放，身体要保持自然放松状态。

其次，执笔的方法要正确。它不仅影响书写速度，还决定了书写效果。用钢笔书写，一般采用三指

> How to Write Chinese Characters

Writing is not only an important way to know Chinese characters but also a vital channel for self-expression. However, it is not easy to learn writing and harder to write well. In the course, one should be confident, patient and never be discouraged. With regard to writing tools, one can use fountain pen, ballpoint pen or pencil, all based on personal preferences. Here illustrates writing by the case of fountain pen.

First of all, right posture is the prerequisite for good writing, which simultaneously can protect eyesight and reduce fatigue. Generally speaking, the writer should keep his head upright or slightly tilted forward, the arms unfolded and flatly put on the desk, the feet naturally separated on the ground, the body erect and in a relaxed state.

执笔法：大拇指和食指从左右两个角度夹住笔杆，指头离笔尖约3厘米，中指垫在笔杆下面；无名指和小拇指自然弯曲，伸向手心。五指自然用力，手掌不要握实。

掌握了正确的书写姿势，便可以临摹字帖了。选择好的字帖尤为重要，书写者首先要选择自己喜爱的字帖。一般来说，初学者应选择

Secondly, one should hold the pen in the right way, which not only affects the writing speed, but decides the writing effect. When writing with a fountain pen, man generally adopts three-finger holding method. The thumb and index finger press against the shaft—about 3cm from the pen tip—from the right and left sides. Meanwhile the middle finger cushions the shaft. The ring finger and little finger naturally bend towards the palm. All five fingers give force with ease rather than hold the pen too firmly.

Learning the right and proper writing posture, one also needs frequent imitation of copybooks. Choosing a good copybook is quite important. One may select his copybook according to personal preference, but the copybook must conform to writing standard. Generally, beginners should choose a copybook in regular script. It features large character, clear calligraphy and no strong personal touch which might affect the beginners' writing habits. In the copying process,

● 书写者的正确姿势
姿势要端正，保持自然。头部微垂，双臂放于桌上支撑身体。
Right Posture for Writers
One should maintain an upright and natural posture with head slightly lowered and arms unfolded on the desk to support the body.

食指在上，向内侧用力。
The index finger stays upwards and presses inward.

拇指在下，向内侧用力。
The thumb stays downwards and also presses inward.

中指垫在笔杆下方，与拇指、食指一起夹住笔杆。
The middle finger cushions the lower part of the shaft and presses against the shaft along with the thumb and the index finger.

- 三指执笔法
  Three-finger Holding Method

楷体字帖，字要大，书写要清晰，且不能带有太强的个人色彩，这会影响初学者的写字习惯。临摹的过程中要遵照汉字笔画结构、偏旁部首的规范写法。

下面介绍点、横、竖、撇、捺、提、折、钩的基本写法：

one should adhere to the writing norms for strokes and radicals.

In the following I will introduce writing ways of the eight basic strokes, respectively, dot, horizontal stroke, vertical stroke, left-falling stroke, right-falling stroke, right-rising stroke, turning stroke and hook.

笔画名称 Stroke Name	笔画 Stroke Shape	写法 Way of Writing	例字 Sample Character
点 Dot	丶	短点的书写起笔要轻，收笔要重，短促有力；长点的书写速度相对较慢，书写要稳。 To write a short and forceful dot, one starts the stroke softly and closes heavily, whereas for a long dot, one writes slowly and steadily.	文 Wen (literary)
横 Horizontal Stroke	一	横画的书写行笔较快，收笔要重，写得要稳。同一个字中横画长短不一。 Horizontal stroke moves fast and steadily in the middle and closes heavily. Horizontal strokes in one character can vary in length.	天 Tian (heaven)
竖 Vertical Stroke	丨	竖画起笔较重，行笔向下力度逐渐减轻，一般收笔较重；当竖画为汉字的最后一笔时，收笔宜尖。 The vertical stroke starts heavily and gradually reduces in strength as moving downward, but closes heavily. When vertical stroke becomes the finishing touch of the character, the end of the stroke should be pointed.	中 Zhong (middle)
撇 Left-falling Stroke	丿	撇画起笔较重，收笔较轻，需要注意撇画的长短和方向的不同。 Left-falling stroke starts heavily and closes softly. One should pay attention to the length and direction of different left-falling strokes.	后 Hou (after)

捺 Right-falling Stroke	㇏	捺画下笔较轻，行笔向右下由轻到重，收尾处顿笔向右水平方向提笔出锋。收笔要尖。 The right-falling stroke starts softly and then becomes heavier as moving down towards the right corner. By the end of the stroke, first pause, then move horizontally to the right, and finally raise the pen to make a tip.	入 *Ru* (enter)
提 Right-rising Stroke	㇀	提画起笔较重，然后由重到轻向右上行笔，出锋收笔。写得要有力。 Right-rising stroke starts heavily, then reduces in strength as moving towards the upper right corner and finally closes the stroke forcefully with a tip.	汗 *Han* (sweat)
折 Turning Stroke	㇆	折画为组合型笔画，转折处的书写速度要放慢，先顿再折。 Turning stroke is a combination of strokes. At the turning point, the stroke moves slowly, then pauses and turns.	乃 *Nai* (therefore)
钩 Hook	㇚	钩画为组合型笔画，需结合其他笔画的写法。书写时要有力度。 Hook is also a combination of strokes and should be written with force. You can refer to the writing ways of other strokes.	字 *Zi* (character)